I0520593

SLAYED BY A WOMAN

SLAYED BY A WOMAN

ASHTON A BOHANNON

Contents

Preamble

Christians are on a quest doing exploits and taking ground from our enemy. One of the ways we succeed in our mission is through leadership. Throughout history into the current age, there have been attempts to pollute the sanctuary and attempts to purify it. Leaders who remain awake and active soldiers on the battlefield of our God work daily to keep the temple holy and consecrated unto the Lord. Demonically inspired leaders, likewise, work until they are worn out to inspire an impure worship among the people. These wolves in sheep's clothing, try to corrupt God's house, in the name of religion.

God's children operate under the supernatural, invigorating power of God. We continue pressing forward in the battles of life when others quit. We work diligently under a higher power to purify the saints through preaching and teaching the pure Word of the Lord. We strengthen the Church, train new believers, and remove polluted people and things from our places of worship, so God's will can be done on the earth as it is in heaven. We cast out all evil from our worship so that the true sheep of the flock remain safe. A wolf left unchecked and unbothered will do damage, but a wolf identified and confronted will be driven away from the people because it knows it doesn't stand a chance in the fight.

We find this truth spoken by the prophet Daniel:

And armed forces of his shall appear [in the holy land] and they shall pollute the sanctuary, the [spiritual] stronghold, and shall take away the continual [daily burnt offering]; and they shall set up [in the sanctuary] the abomination that astonishes and makes desolate [probably an altar to a pagan god]. And such as violate the covenant he shall pervert and seduce with flatteries, but the people who know their God shall prove themselves strong and shall stand firm and do exploits [for God] (Daniel 11:31-32, Amplified).

1

God's Justice System

Children of God operate in power and hold supernatural resources because of the spiritual kingdom they belong to. Once they are saved, God's children are given an access key authorizing them to come boldly into the presence of the Lord, to access the heavenly realms. After we accept Jesus Christ as our Savior, we are eligible to receive the kingdom's resources and advantages. God's people have supernatural powers and assistance the rest of the world simply does not have because they share the keys powerful enough to unlock all things within the heavens and the earth.

Access keys are special: They open doors. When we take possession of an access key, we can go through the doors that others cannot. Access keys can be to a room, a building, or even to a larger establishment, but they always permit people access to something not accessible to the public. Behind the locked gates or doors there is an entire world and an entire destination, separate from the rest of the world, and it is always valuable and special, set aside for those who possess the key.

The keys we have to God's kingdom represent our privilege and rights as key holders. The keys separate who is allowed into holy places under the holy anointing and those who are not. Although the Lord is no respecter of persons and wants all to come into the kingdom, the unfortunate reality is many people choose to reject the invitation for salvation and the anointing. And without the keys of salvation and the anointing, people restrict their own access to the magnificent supernatural realm, denying themselves the ample resources they greatly need to thrive and prosper.

Once we are saved and are living in the kingdom of God, God wants us to intercede for the weak and the lost through our leadership and our prayers. Without God's wisdom and the acceptance of the truth, people are hungry, thirsty, and perishing in their sin or ignorance. As God's ambassadors, we are urged by God to intercede for those who are still lost and deceived, living under the dominion and control of the Evil One. We are told to give sight to the blind, open the ears of the deaf, and to restore lives. Matthew 10:8 explains, *"Heal the sick, raise the dead, cleanse the lepers, cast out demons. Freely you have received, freely give."* (NIV)

All believers will continually need to be fed and recharged through the knowledge and understanding of the Word. Being saved is just the beginning. There is so much God has available for His people. Praying and working towards winning souls for the kingdom is the number one priority of the Church, but Jesus told us to go into deeper revelation and knowledge. He instructed us to press forward into a higher dimension and understanding as His disciples.

The mature church must also learn to work together to achieve the mission of Christ through the care, support, and kindness to the other saints. We must take responsibility for our lives and intercede on behalf of the lives of those God has placed around us in God's house.

First Timothy 2:1-4 tells us, *"First of all, then, I urge that petitions (specific requests), prayers, intercessions (prayers for others) and thanksgivings be offered on behalf of all people, for kings and all who are in [positions of] high authority, so that we may live a peaceful and quiet life in all godliness and dignity. This [kind of praying] is good and acceptable and pleasing in the sight of God our Savior, who desires all people to be saved and to come to the knowledge and recognition of the [divine] truth."* (AMPC)

The only way we can edify the church or see lost souls come into the light and be freed from the demonic realm is to operate in power and in authority from heaven. In our own strength, we are incapable of opposing the demonic realm and setting the captive free. To see freedom and breakthrough, and to fight the evil forces in the earth, we must obey every part of God's Word. This means loving people and praying for their salvation and their betterment. It means standing up for justice and truth at all costs, even when the hearer doesn't like the message. God commanded us to preach and teach to the world, and even the enemies of God deserve to be told the truth, so they are given a chance to repent.

Pontius Pilate the governor of Judaea was warned by his wife to not harm Jesus. God gave Pilate's wife the knowledge and information she needed to convey the message to her husband. Pilate knew the truth and there are witnesses confirming his knowledge of the truth, but he still remained committed to the path of destruction and evil. Matthew 27:19 tells us, *"While he was seated on the judgment seat, his wife sent him a message, saying, "Have nothing to do with that righteous and innocent Man; for last night I suffered greatly in a dream because of Him.""* (NIV)

Jesus assured us that we would do greater works than He did. He promised us we would have a helper; a force of God to assist us in our mission. John 14:12 says, *"I assure you and most solemnly say to you, anyone who believes in Me [as Savior] will also do the things that I do; and he will do even greater things than these [in extent and outreach], because I am going to the Father."* (AMPC) Christians who know their identity, purpose, and call operate in power and in authority as Jesus operated during His time on the earth. Miracles and supernatural things will arise from their lives and ministries , because God is true to His word.

As we perform the works of God and walk as we are called to walk, all people will be able to see we are unlike the rest of the world. If we blend in, and are not bold, strong and different, we are in danger of losing our salt, and becoming good for nothing in God's kingdom. If we refuse to treat all people with kindness, love, and Christian virtue, we become unfit for service. Moses was kind to Pharaoh, as he warned him of impending judgment if he didn't change his evil ways. True love warns people of their sin. Godly love corrects and rebukes all kinds of evil.

First Peter 2:9 declares, *"But you are a chosen race, a royal priesthood, a dedicated nation, [God's] own purchased, special people, that you may set forth the wonderful deeds and display the virtues and perfections of Him Who called you out of darkness into His marvelous light."* (AMPC)

Kindness doesn't mean servitude or submission to evil. We can be loving, kind, and respectful to people without ever changing our mission or our proclamation of the truth. The most loving and kind thing a Christian can do for another person is to tell them the truth, regardless of how they receive it. We know we are doing God's will and work when we do this, because without the light of the truth, people will never be set free.

The Church will prosper during this last season of time despite being hated and disliked by many for our commitment to the gospel message. Regardless of who does or does not like us, the Church will continue to take ground, and we will conquer the enemy forces. God didn't design His church to be trampled or walked on by man or devils. God sent Jesus Christ to the earth to die for our sins, so we could occupy and fulfill His plan for the last days we live in.

Today, as we are living in the church age, the final period of time, we will prepare the earth for Jesus Christ's return and ultimate destruction of the enemy forces, because it is what we have been called to do.

Serving God ensures we are living with the blessing, as serving the devil ensures people will receive the curse. As we choose to partner with God, we will be noticeably different from the world, because it is our covenant inheritance. All Christians tread over top of those who refuse to comply to God's standards and His sovereign Word, because

God decreed sowing and reaping, blessing or cursing for every one of his creations.

Malachi 3:18 tells us, *"Then you will again see the difference between the righteous and the wicked, between those who serve God and those who do not."* The Lord of Heaven's Armies says, *"The day of judgment is coming, burning like a furnace. On that day the arrogant and the wicked will be burned up like straw. They will be consumed—roots, branches, and all. "But for you who fear my name, the Sun of Righteousness will rise with healing in his wings. And you will go free, leaping with joy like calves let out to pasture. On the day when I act, you will tread upon the wicked as if they were dust under your feet," says the Lord of Heaven's Armies."* (NIV)

When we interact with people, the saved and unsaved, there must be proof of the Holy Spirit living within us. We need to testify and witness to the world about Jesus Christ and His blood that was shed for our sins. The wicked won't be with us in heaven, so Malachi wasn't referring to our future there.

Malachi perceived in the Spirit that the Holy Spirit would be poured out upon the Church on the earth, and he perceived that this outpouring would transform the world in the last days, impacting both the saved and the unsaved. He was telling all of us what the death, burial, and resurrection of Jesus Christ would do for the members of the church age church under the new covenant.

It is intentional that Malachi is the last book of the Old Testament. This position indicates to us that the old covenant was leaving and the new was coming. The Church today is fulfilling the book of Malachi. We are moving in power and in the anointing like never before, and through our words, actions, and outward witness, we can testify we have been purchased and bought at a price, and we serve a living God.

Some Christians want to blend in with society. The desire to be loved, accepted, and tolerated by the world is an unreasonable desire as a Christian. Jesus said being loved by the world wasn't our path as His followers. In John 15:18-19 He says, *"If the world hates you, keep in mind that it hated me first. If you belonged to the world, it would love you as its own. As it is, you do not belong to the world, but I have chosen you out of the world. That is why the world hates you."* (NIV)

The Church is the most powerful institution in the world. With Christ's help, it moves nations, people, and all spiritual beings living and operating within the world around us. If Satan himself is a ruler of the world and we remove and trample him, we are operating within a higher kingdom and under a higher power in which all people and all spiritual beings are subject. From the lowest to the highest position in the kingdom of God, we are still higher than all evil.

Spiritual leaders, who are explained within scripture as spiritual mothers and fathers, must walk in their position with honor and dignity. Through positive, loving, and Christlike behaviors toward others, spiritual leaders empower the saved and the unsaved to seek a relationship with God, repent from sin, and become more like Jesus every single day. The Lord calls powerful, anointed leaders to raise up and train an army of people to advance the gospel and the mission of the Church. He commands us to not neglect teaching the full counsel of the Word. Jeremiah 48:10 explains, *"Cursed are those who refuse to do the Lord's work, who hold back their swords from shedding blood!"* (NIV)

The Church has a mission unlike the mission of the world at large. Jesus explains, *"The Spirit of Truth, whom the world cannot receive [and take to its heart] because it does not see Him or know Him, but you know Him because He (the Holy Spirit) remains with you continually and will be in you."* (John 14:17, Amplified). Since the Holy Spirit was poured out on the earth, the Church has walked effortlessly in the supernatural as Jesus did when He walked the earth, because we have a helper from heaven. The Holy Spirit's works with us to provide hope and healing for a world that desperately needs it.

The covenant we made with God when we accepted Jesus Christ as our Savior has many precious promises and guarantees. Outlined in it are expectations and obligations we need to fulfill. Covenants are agreements — binding promises with obligations and commitments set forth. When God gave His covenant He intended to keep every single part of it. As we are in covenant with God, we should aim to be like Him and keep our side of the covenant in every way too.

While many people know the commands about reaching the lost and helping the hurting in the world, some church people fail to uphold their promise to honor and train the members of Christ's body within the house of God. It is critical that we live in peace with each other, and seek the best for one another, as Christ said: *"So, when you are offering your gift at the altar you there remember that your brother has any [grievance] against you, Leave your gift at the altar and go. First make peace with your brother, and then come back and present your gift* (Matthew 5:23-24, Amplified).

God's standard is higher than man's standards and His goal in the courtroom is to always rule on the side of pure justice for all the people in the world, under all circumstances. Most of the world's legal systems operate under the premises of justice, integrity, and freedom. These powerful institutions often promote change, protection, and assistance for people while they are living on earth; and they are only man made organizations. In man's courtroom, if there is an adherence to laws and the contracts made promoting and upholding freedom for all, then how much more should the Church advocate for these principles and truths?

Christians are to uphold the laws of God. We are to enforce and advocate for justice and truth in our daily lives. As people enter contracts/covenants, the court system can uphold the agreement and require the individual to be accountable for their behavior, either good or bad. A marriage cannot easily be dissolved in the courts, because the marriage is upheld by a legal document. In legal proceedings, contracts and covenants carry weight because they are being held in place with the backing of the legal infrastructure.

A lifestyle outside of Jesus Christ can never be holy and meet God's standards. For this reason, we all must ask Jesus for forgiveness and accept His sacrifice, if we are going to be pardoned and forgiven for our crimes. All people are born sinners, and if we have never publicly confessed and testified to our sin nature, then we will not be eligible for forgiveness on the day of judgment. Romans 10:9 teaches, *"because if you acknowledge and confess with your mouth that Jesus is Lord [recognizing His power, authority, and majesty as God], and believe in your heart that God raised Him from the dead, you will be saved."* (AMPC)

And while the sinner may be unable to meet the standards, this is not true for the saint. Christians have the power to do what is just. They have the tools they need to live a holy life. First Peter 1:16 teaches us what it means to be a follower of Jesus: *"for it is written: "Be holy, because I am holy.""* (NIV) Christians do not live outside of the covenant. We live and dwell within it following all of the laws of God as an example of righteousness.

God allows people to violate the covenant and to walk outside of His commands, but they are never free from the consequences of their choices. People can commit robbery even though stealing is against the law, but once the crime has occurred, the judge has legal grounds to punish and sentence for the crime. There are both current and eternal consequences for the choices we make while we are living on the earth.

Those who choose to never enter a covenant with the Lord through salvation in Christ, are inherently guilty because of the inheritance of sin, the sin nature all of humanity is born with. Romans 5:12 says, *"Therefore, just as sin entered the world through one man, and death through sin, and in this way death came to all people, because all sinned—"* (NIV).

Fornication is the association and intimate relationship with another whom we are not married too. As Adam and Eve joined themselves to the Devil through their unholy union with sin, they became cursed and so did their descendants. People are joined to the unholy gods until we die to our former nature and marry and become one in a covenant with Jesus Christ. We must leave the family of sin and come into the family of Christ by joining ourselves to Him. When we accept Jesus, we die and are reborn as a new creation. *Put to death, therefore, whatever belongs to your earthly nature: sexual immorality, impurity, lust, evil desires and greed, which is idolatry* (Colossians 3:5, NIV).

Being out of a covenant relationship with the Lord condemns mankind of fornication, because, through Adam and Eve, humans chose to engage in an intimate relationship with the devil and the demonic realm. This decision had consequences for future generations. Through choosing to yoke themselves in an unholy intimate union, the children of future generations became cursed. This changes only when they consciously decide to change their life's course by accepting Jesus Christ as their Savior. Fornication is distinct from adultery where infidelity occurs within the marriage relationship as opposed to outside of it.

Entering the covenant relationship with the Lord permits us access to the latter rain as spoken of by Malachi. We leave the curse, and we join the family of God. In our new family we are given keys to the kingdom of heaven, and keys to rule on the earth. We get the blessings and the privileges given to Jesus, because we are one with Him. Christians are spiritual beings living on the earth. We are not from this world; we originate in heaven.

And He raised us up together with Him [when we believed], and seated us with Him in the heavenly places, [because we are] in Christ Jesus, [and He did this] so that in the ages to come He might [clearly] show the immeasurable and unsurpassed riches of His grace in [His] kindness toward us in Christ Jesus [by providing for our redemption] (Ephesians 2:6-7, Amplified).

Responsibility comes with the blessings of God. To partake in the good things of God we become far more responsible. Outlined within the covenant with God through Christ's redemption, we are expected to be faithful to Him. As we do our part, He will always do His. When people are not faithful, they become intimate with devils again, in essence cheating on the Lord. Adultery is the sin of a married person who engages in intimate relationships with someone other than their spouse. The Lord tells us when the members of the Church are unfaithful and they sleep with devils, they will be rightfully judged and condemned for their misconduct in the marriage.

Exodus 20:5 teaches, *"You shall not bow down to them or worship them; for I, the Lord your God, am a jealous God, punishing the children for the sin of the parents to the third and fourth generation of those who hate me."* (NIV) The only hope for the man or woman caught in the act of spiritual fornication or adultery is true repentance, a turning from sin, and a heart committed to the Lord and only Him, from now until eternity. When God permits us access into His heart, His kingdom, and He gives us His love, let us not take it for granted. Let us not be unfaithful to Him. Let us long to be loyal and faithful to the King of Kings.

Ezekiel 23:2-3

The prophet Ezekiel speaks about this kind of spiritual immorality.

"Son of man, there were two women (Israel and Judah), the daughters of one mother (the united kingdom); and they prostituted themselves in Egypt. From their youth they were grossly immoral; in that place their breasts were embraced and their virgin bosom was grasped. (AMPC)

Ezekiel 23:36-39

"Therefore this is what the Sovereign Lord says: Since you have forgotten me and turned your back on me, you must bear the consequences of your lewdness and prostitution." The Lord said to me: "Son of man, will you judge Oholah and Oholibah? Then confront them with their detestable practices, for they have committed adultery and blood is on their hands. They committed adultery with their idols; they even sacrificed their children, whom they bore to me, as food for them. They have also done this to me: At that same time they defiled my sanctuary and desecrated my Sabbaths. On the very day they sacrificed their children to their idols, they entered my sanctuary and desecrated it. That is what they did in my house." (AMPC)

2

Created in the Image of God Almighty

In the United States, a legal dispute and demonic ideology separated white Americans and black Americans by their racial identity — until 1954. White and black Americans could not attend the same schools, ride in the same train cars, or eat in the same restaurants. These regulations limited the freedoms of all Americans, and they harmed America at large because they were rooted in sin. Jealousy, hate, and injustice are unholy, and whenever these characteristics arise, they come from the devourer.

When laws are enforced to harm large groups of people, the devil has succeeded in strategizing and executing an intentional plot to destroy people and their civilization. Satan wants to infiltrate the justice systems of mankind, causing large scale chaos and damage. He wants to dominate these powerful systems so he can influence large groups of people. The more influence and power Satan can enforce at the hands of men, the more he can control the earth.

Segregation, although better than slavery, was one way Satan affected masses of people. Segregation was still unjust and harmful. At the core of segregation was hatred and division aimed at degradation of the soul and the spirit. When black Americans were treated as inferior, even when assured equal value in the eyes of the law and society, they knew they were being limited their full freedom and access. Many chose to stand up and fight against the tyranny and injustice of the system because being segregated was promoting demonstrated inferiority, regardless of what the people in power or the society at large deemed fair and equal.

The Fourteenth Amendment of the United States' Constitution decrees that all Americans have protection under American laws because of their identity as Americans. Section 1 of this amendment states "All persons born or naturalized in the United States, and subject to the jurisdiction thereof, are citizens of the United States and of the state wherein they reside. No state shall make or enforce any law which shall abridge the privileges or immunities of citizens of the United States; nor shall any state deprive any person of life, liberty, or property, without due process of law; nor deny to any person within its jurisdiction the equal protection of the laws." (The United States Senate).

When segregation laws were challenged by a man named Homer Plessy, the Supreme Court refused to change the laws on segregation. This failure to change the laws was a failure within the American courts because by law, segregation laws were unjust and a violation of the Fourteenth Amendment. The people ruling in the 7-1 decision against Plessy said they upheld the constitutionality of Louisiana's train car segregation laws because there was no law violation, when indeed there was.

Homer Plessy was of mixed race, being both white and black, so he purchased a "whites only" first-class ticket to ride in a train car in Louisiana. When he was questioned about his race, he was honest and was forcibly thrown out of the train and arrested. Despite being correct in the eyes of God to challenge the state and the federal law, the people of the local, state, and national government refused to acknowledge Plessy as a rightful heir to equal rights and treatment enforced through the policies and laws of the land.

An inaccurate interpretation of the law is Satan's tool he uses in secular and religious circles. Satan will speak Scripture to believers, but it is an inaccurate interpretation. He does this so he can convince believers to sin against God while wrongfully justifying their deeds. He will also use the courts, the leaders, and the government to enact laws that are unjust or unholy so he can control societies and people willing to bow to or unquestionably go along with the demons behind his operation.

As in the days of segregation in America, today, many women within the Church are told they are second class citizens in the body of Christ, as black Americans were in America. In many churches women are denied access to their privileges and rights and are told to separate themselves from the men in places of leadership or other inappropriate settings. In many religious circles, women are denied access to the rights and privileges owed to all Christians and descendants of Abraham, because of their gender that was assigned to them by God. Women have been persecuted, some unto death, as well as excommunicated from their church for their refusal to comply to the rules and regulations of denominations or church groups that are resistant to grant equal access to women.

In the 1600s, women were killed in America after being accused of being witches. While some of these women may indeed have been involved in demonic acts or with witchcraft, many people attest that not all the women were. Women may have been prophetic or seeing into the spirit realm, and they may have been Christians who were involving themselves in the religious sphere dominated by men and thus assumed to be of the devil. And for this, they were hated and killed.

When anointed women want to honor God, preach the Word and heal, help, and deliver people, others will rise to try to keep them down. Evil spirits have operated in a similar manner throughout history. The same hateful, vile, and disgusting spirits roam the earth looking for a new target and a new age to try to degrade those who God loves.

Satan has persuaded some to believe they are right in abusing women within the Church, as he has done for thousands of years. These individuals feel justified in their rulings, and they feel as if they are "right" in the eyes of the law. Yet, as in the case of Plessy, men and women who are terribly misled and operating outside of justice may uphold their stance and decision even when this decision is not backed by authority in heaven. Most Pharisees and other religious leaders never repented of putting Jesus or any of the other prophets of God to death, but their lack of repentance will be held to their record on judgment day.

Sound doctrine preached by Jesus Christ permits all men, women, races, and nations to serve the Lord and receive the same benefits for their service. Yet many hold onto false teachings and doctrines of devils teaching and preaching a different gospel. Galatians 3:28-29 explains, *"There is [now no distinction] neither Jew nor Greek, there is neither slave nor free, there is not male and female; for you are all one in Christ Jesus. And if you belong to Christ [are in Him Who is Abraham's Seed], then you are Abraham's offspring and [spiritual] heirs according to promise."* (AMPC)

The blessing of Abraham is available for all who believe through faith. Temporal classifications of gender, race, financial standing, family origin, or other social constraints are invalid and non scriptural disqualifiers. The laws of God assert *"For in Christ Jesus you are all sons of God through faith. For as many [of you] as were baptized into Christ [into a spiritual union and communion with Christ, the Anointed One, the Messiah] have put on (clothed yourselves with) Christ."* (AMPC)

The formal definition of a distinction in the *Oxford Dictionary* is the separation of things or people into different groups according to their attributes or characteristics. Was God confused when He said: *"There is now no distinction neither Jew or Greek, slave or free, or male or female?"* Or are we simply in need of deeper revelation and clarification about sound doctrine and what it means to be in Christ Jesus? If there is no distinction, then there is no separation and classification of rights and privileges.

Many people assert that the right to preach should not be accessible to women. These people view preaching and teaching the Word of God as a privilege only men can access. The key and the privilege to the realm of preaching and teaching are held in their pocket, and they refuse to allow anyone into the "train car" if they don't fit their qualifications. Yet these men and women have been greatly deceived. They have misinterpreted the Scriptures, and they have the blood of the women they persecute and stone on their hands.

First Timothy 1:9-10 says, *"understanding the fact that law is not enacted for the righteous person [the one in right standing with God], but for lawless and rebellious people, for the ungodly and sinful, for the irreverent and profane, for those who kill their fathers or mothers, for murderers, for sexually immoral persons, for homosexuals, for kidnappers and slave traders, for liars, for perjurers—and for whatever else is contrary to sound doctrine."* (AMPC)

The law wasn't meant to hold women down. It was to teach proper behavior to those who are perishing. Do we suppose God gives women wisdom to simply be silent and to watch the world around her go to hell? Do we suppose the Lord created half of the army of the Lord to remain dormant in the mission against the gates of hell when the time is short and people need to be saved? Would God create a spiritual family and want there to be spiritual fathers, and not spiritual mothers as well? Certainly not!

Women were created by God to work alongside their brothers. Although women are unique and are not men, they are equal to men in their rights and their privileges from heaven. As stated before, we have all been given the same access key, and we have the same rights and privileges. While it may be true that blacks and whites have different skin colors, these colors do not determine value or ability or worth of the individual. Likewise, women deserve equal access, opportunity, and love from their brothers and their sisters in the church. They were created to receive equal access and protection under the covenant.

Consider the example of Esther. When she became queen, an evil man named Haman, an agent of Satan and his associates, attempted to use gender and race as a dividing force. The judges and the assistants of the king determined women were to be punished for the disobedience of Queen Vashti, who was the queen before Esther took the throne. Vashti was abused and mistreated, and she was excommunicated from her position because she didn't bow to an unholy mandate to appear before the king. Abusive male headship and assumed superiority and dominance led to more problems for the king and for the people of the land, and Satan was behind it all.

King Ahasuerus, Vashti and Esther's husband, divorced his wife out of selfishness and personal gain. His actions demonstrated man's plan apart from God, as Scripture clearly outlines that divorce is a violation of the law. King Ahasuerus took man's advice, not Gods, and these men twisted and used the law to violate the rights of the women of the land. This law was harmful not only to Vashti, but to many women, demonstrating how Satan targets the leaders and uses the law to trickle the mandates down to the people.

Esther 1:19-22 says, *"If it pleases the king, let a royal command go forth from him and let it be written among the laws of the Persians and Medes, so that it may not be changed, that Vashti is to [be divorced and] come no more before King Ahasuerus; and let the king give her royal position to another who is better than she. So when the king's decree is made and proclaimed throughout all his kingdom, extensive as it is, all wives will give honor to their husbands, high and low. This advice pleased the king and the princes, and the king did what Memucan proposed. He sent letters to all the royal provinces, to each in its own script and to every people in their own language, saying that every man should rule in his own house and speak there in the language of his own people. [If he had foreign wives, let them learn his language.]* (AMPC)

King Ahasuerus did not have a reason to divorce his wife. Nonetheless, following the suggestions of the men around him, he perpetrated evil in the sight of God and justified his decision. In those days, it was common for kings to receive advice from spiritual leaders and judges, and these men were expected to provide honest and just guidance for the king. In fact, that was their primary job. Nonetheless, in this circumstance, the judges and other advisors to the king were fools, void of God's truth, and endowed with the lies of Satan, calling evil good and good evil.

Jesus makes this teaching clear. *"It has been said, 'Anyone who divorces his wife must give her a certificate of divorce.' But I tell you that anyone who divorces his wife, except for sexual immorality, makes her the victim of adultery, and anyone who marries a divorced woman commits adultery"* (Matthew 5:31, NIV).

Esther's cousin, Mordeci, a wise, God-fearing man, realized it was an advantage to not focus on or gender or race. He realized he was in a spiritual battle, not a physical one. By looking into the spirit, Mordeci perceived that God was going to use someone to help His people. Mordeci didn't disqualify Esther because of her gender. He realized she could be the voice that saved them. Mordeci trained and raised Esther to be a God-fearing woman, unashamed of her identity but intelligent enough to ignore it in the battle with her enemy.

Esther 2:20 explains, *"Now Esther had not yet revealed her nationality or her people, for she obeyed Mordecai's command to her [to fear God and execute His commands] just as when she was being brought up by him."* (AMPC) Focusing on the battle instead of her gender or her race, Esther defeated her enemies and brought deliverance to God's people. The same will happen for us today. When we focus on God and our mission, and we pay no mind to our characteristics of gender, race, or nationality, we will slay the enemy and win the victory for the Lord. And Satan can't do anything to stop it.

Pay no mind to those who use gender, race, and other characteristics to destroy and tear down what God wants to build up. Don't be quiet and retreat in fear. The Lord wants us to go forward in faith. Recognize the enemies' strategy and refuse to comply with it. Step out in obedience to your God, and He will reward you. He will use you to do great and mighty things.

God doesn't care if we are a man or a woman, and He doesn't care about our race or background. He cares about our faith. When we believe we can do all things through Him, we will.

Esther 4:14 tells us how critical this is: *"For if you keep silent at this time, relief and deliverance shall arise for the Jews from elsewhere, but you and your father's house will perish. And who knows but perhaps you have come to the kingdom for such a time as this and for this very occasion?"* (AMPC)

3

Jael & Deborah: Women Moving Forward

Discerning the time we are living in is essential. If you don't realize you are living in the last hour, carrying the most powerful weapon of heaven, you won't receive what God has for you and others who would be blessed by your ministry. The older generation must be diligent to train in the ways of the Lord, and the younger generation must be responsible and receptive to the call.

"Therefore, be on the alert [be prepared and ready], for you do not know the day nor the hour [when the Son of Man will come]. "For it is just like a man who was about to take a journey, and he called his servants together and entrusted them with his possessions. To one he gave five talents, to another, two, and to another, one, each according to his own ability; and then he went on his journey. The one who had received the five talents went at once and traded with them, and he [made a profit and] gained five more. Likewise the one who had two [made a profit and] gained two more. But the one who had received the one went and dug a hole in the ground and hid his master's money" (Matthew 25:13-18, Amplified).

In the parable of the talents, Jesus instructed His people to use the talents and the gifts given to them. Gifts are seeds that have been given to individuals for them to be used purposefully. People will be accountable for the seed they have been given and there are no exceptions. Seeds are supposed to produce fruit and bring forth something that is beneficial to another living thing. And our seed is our key to our harvest.

A good tomato plant is refreshing, filling, and beneficial to the farmer and to others who can eat its fruit. In the same way, believers are to plant seeds that benefit us and the world around us. We are designed to bring life and restoration to the people, places, and things we encounter during our life on the earth. We can change lives, restore cities, and revive nations by leading people to the Vine and demonstrating the truths of the Bible.

Christians are restoration experts. We can take a person/plant that has been dead and connect it to the source of life. We can restore desolate places and bring hope, healing, and functionality back into the man, woman, or child. People, places, or things that are destroyed, abandoned, and left for dead can be brought back to the fullness of life if we involve ourselves in the situation.

Christians should never go into bad places and be changed by evil. The goal of the Christian mission is to restore and revive, not to succumb and survive. Isaiah describes this: *"Then they will rebuild the ancient ruins, They will raise up and restore the former desolations; And they will renew the ruined cities, The desolations (deserted settlements) of many generations"* (Isaiah 61:4, NIV).

Spiritual restoration is critical. Satan can remain only in the places we allow him to remain. When Christians understand their job and their power from God, they will run to dilapidated things, knowing they can be beautiful again. The ability to see a person, a city, or a situation with hope is the necessary component of seeing transformation. There is no place, person, or situation God can't change and restore as long as people are open to restoration.

The hand of the Lord was on me, and he brought me out by the Spirit of the Lord and set me in the middle of a valley; it was full of bones. He led me back and forth among them, and I saw a great many bones on the floor of the valley, bones that were very dry. He asked me, "Son of man, can these bones live?" I said, "Sovereign Lord, you alone know." Then he said to me, "Prophesy to these bones and say to them, ' 'Dry bones, hear the word of the Lord! This is what the Sovereign Lord says to these bones: I will make breath enter you, and you will come to life.

I will attach tendons to you and make flesh come upon you and cover you with skin; I will put breath in you, and you will come to life. Then you will know that I am the Lord.'" So I prophesied as I was commanded. And as I was prophesying, there was a noise, a rattling sound, and the bones came together, bone to bone. I looked, and tendons and flesh appeared on them and skin covered them, but there was no breath in them. Then he said to me, "Prophesy to the breath; prophesy, son of man, and say to it, 'This is what the Sovereign Lord says: Come, breath, from the four winds and breathe into these slain, that they may live.'" So I prophesied as he commanded me, and breath entered them; they came to life and stood up on their feet—a vast army.

Then he said to me: "Son of man, these bones are the people of Israel. They say, 'Our bones are dried up and our hope is gone; we are cut off.' Therefore prophesy and say to them: 'This is what the Sovereign Lord says: My people, I am going to open your graves and bring you up from them; I will bring you back to the land of Israel. Then you, my people, will know that I am the Lord, when I open your graves and bring you up from them. I will put my Spirit in you and you will live, and I will settle you in your own land. Then you will know that I the Lord have spoken, and I have done it, declares the Lord'" (Ezekiel 37:1-14, NIV).

God, through the establishment of the new blood covenant, restored and brought back the dead. He is and has been raising up an army as He said He would do, ever since the death, burial, and resurrection of Jesus. With the help of the Holy Spirit, we are alive and thriving, attached to the Vine. And God will use us to be restorative in the lives of others. He will partner with us to act like Him as we live here on the earth.

The Church must not be afraid to be the hands and feet of God to this generation. Without our intentional intervention, the next generation will be separate from their Creator, because God gave the job of preaching and teaching the gospel to mankind.

The Church needs restoration, but it also needs innovation to accomplish our mission. Some religious groups have separated themselves from the world too much. Many have become a type of Jonah who flee from Ninevah because they do not want to preach to the people they deem worthless and evil. Yet, the Church is not a cult, and it is not a social club for people who are saved. The Church is the force stopping the devil from dominating the entire world. We are the restrainers of the demonic, and we are partners with God to save the lost and dying world.

Christians are created to be better, not worse, than the people of the world. Christians have supernatural abilities and powers the rest of the world doesn't have. A Christian musician should be far better than their demonic counterpart. Christian authors should show the world they walk in authority and power, and their publications should be far more advanced and thought provoking. These realities then, will draw people to the Church and ultimately salvation, because they see that they are lacking an element in their life without Jesus Christ as their Lord and Savior.

The Lord will give young people and old people ideas and innovations for their life and the lives of those around them. He will show His people new ways of thinking in their fields, so they can be a blessing to the world around them. Restoration, creativity and innovation are gifts that come from heaven. Receive them today and begin to advance the kingdom and get the gospel to all ends of the earth.

The Church of Jesus Christ will not stop restoring dead places and building new things until Jesus comes back. We were made in the image of our Father who restores things and is creative in how He does it. Christians are the head and not the tail. We are above and not beneath. We are the salt of the earth and the power of God at work on the earth to improve humanity. God has given men and women different talents and abilities, because He has a specific talent for each one of us.

The servant in the parable of the talents was afraid to use the talents God gave him, but these talents were his avenue to move forward into his future. Fear instead of faith dominated this servant, and he displeased his master. In the same way, God wants us to use what we have been given. He wants us to be diligent, hardworking, and attentive people. It isn't enough to simply exist and squander our time as Christians. Our lives should be producing and bearing fruit, and there should be evidence of our conversion to Christ.

"The one who had received one talent also came forward, saying, 'Master, I knew you to be a harsh and demanding man, reaping [the harvest] where you did not sow and gathering where you did not scatter seed. So I was afraid [to lose the talent], and I went and hid your talent in the ground. See, you have what is your own.' "But his master answered him, 'You wicked, lazy servant, you knew that I reap [the harvest] where I did not sow and gather where I did not scatter seed. Then you ought to have put my money with the bankers, and at my return I would have received my money back with interest. So take the talent away from him, and give it to the one who has the ten talents' (Matthew 25:24-28, Amplified).

As we are responsible for our lives and we focus on our calling, we will receive our blessings and our promotion. As we prove we are responsible with the little, we will be given more. Matthew 25:22-23 says, *"Also the one who had the two talents came forward, saying, 'Master, you entrusted two talents to me. See, I have [made a profit and] gained two more talents.' His master said to him, 'Well done, good and faithful servant. You have been faithful and trustworthy over a little, I will put you in charge of many things; share in the joy of your master.'"* (AMPC)

Life is a race, and we are expected to run our race with diligence. When we get to heaven, there will be no war and no reason to fight, so fight today and make every day count as if it were your last. First Corinthians 9:24 explains, *"Do you not know that in a race all the runners* compete, but [only] one receives the prize? So run [your race] that you may lay hold [of the prize] and make it yours." (AMPC)

We do not know when our time on earth will run out. Every day, moment, and hour is important, because people need to be saved. James 4:13-14 explains, "Now listen, you who say, "Today or tomorrow we will go to this or that city, spend a year there, carry on business and make money." Why, you do not even know what will happen tomorrow. What is your life? You are a mist that appears for a little while and then vanishes." (NIV)

Deborah, a judge of Israel, lived in a day where society was struggling from their disobedience to God. Poor decisions brought suffering on the people of the land. God permitted Deborah to speak for Him, and her obedience to God encouraged other people. Deborah's faith encouraged another woman, Jael, and through an innovative approach God worked with two women to bring hope, deliverance, and restoration to His people. The divine timing working in these women's lives was incredible, as it was orchestrated by God, not man and thus it brought perfect deliverance.

"Blessed and worthy of praise be the God and Father of our Lord Jesus Christ, who has blessed us with every spiritual blessing in the heavenly realms in Christ just as [in His love] He chose us in Christ [actually selected us for Himself as His own] before the foundation of the world, so that we would be holy [that is, consecrated, set apart for Him, purpose-driven] and blameless in His sight. In love" (Ephesians 1:3-4, Amplified).

Like Deborah and Jael, we were chosen to lead and deliver our generation. Our talents, abilities, and personalities were foreknown by God. We were hand-picked and given certain capabilities so we could change the world around us for the kingdom of our God. Men and women can't dictate our destiny, because it was written before the foundations of the world.

Yet making an impact for God and His kingdom is a decision we make, and it won't happen by accident. Everyone has a choice to run their race or to sit on the sidelines watching someone else run. And while many choose to be a spectator, many choose to be a player. Judges 5:2 says, *"For the leaders who took the lead in Israel, for the people who offered themselves willingly, bless the Lord!"*

Deborah arose as a mother in Israel; she chose to get up and work for the Lord. The villages were unoccupied and rulers ceased in Israel until you arose—you, Deborah, arose—a mother in Israel (Judges 5:7, Amplified).

Deborah's decision to rise and harken to the voice of God saved lives of the people living around her. Her decision allowed her to partner with God to see people's lives transformed. Judges 5:12 says, *"Awake, awake, Deborah! Awake, awake, utter a song! Arise, Barak, and lead away your captives, you son of Abinoam."* (AMPC)

As Deborah received blessing and honor for joining in the battle, others were cursed for refusing to join the Lord's battle. *"Curse Meroz, said the messenger of the Lord. Curse bitterly its inhabitants, because they came not to the help of the Lord, to the help of the Lord against the mighty"* (Judges 5:3, Amplified)! Our choices determine our outcomes in life. A choice to hide your talent, or to withdraw from a fight, elicits the curse. Conversely, a choice to engage and perform God's work in faith elicits a blessing.

Deborah's faith and obedience to God inspired other women. As Deborah worked for God, she encouraged another woman to work alongside of her. Jael, a heroine, stepped out in faith and used her talent to destroy the works of the enemy and put an end to the war involving God's people. Jael delivered God's army from the enemy forces, by utilizing her skills in combination with her faith, but no doubt she had been trained by the actions of Deborah.

Judges 5:24-27 explains, *"Blessed above women shall Jael, the wife of Heber the Kenite, be; blessed shall she be above women in the tent. [Sisera] asked for water, and she gave [him] milk; she brought him curds in a lordly dish. She put her [left] hand to the tent pin, and her right hand to the workmen's hammer. And with the wooden hammer she smote Sisera, she smote his head, yes, she struck and pierced his temple. He sank, he fell, he lay still at her feet. At her feet he sank, he fell; where he sank, there he fell—dead!"* (AMPC)

Jael was accustomed to putting up tents and was familiar with the process of using tent pegs. She was also accustomed to serving food, providing nourishment and comfort for those around her. When Jael noticed her enemy approaching, she realized God would help her to defeat him, through her unique talents. In faith, Jael soothed a Canaanite general Sisera by providing him with milk.

Jael's story demonstrates the intentionality behind the operations of heaven. God knew Jael would be born and trained in the season of life she needed to be. He knew she was going to be used to help His army. He was aware that the enemy would disregard her as a potential threat, and He used this as an innovative and creative advantage in the war against evil. As the general laid down his weapons in her presence, Jael drove a tent spike through his head, and she won the war for God's people, using her talent God gave her.

The Bible tells us women are the weaker vessel, and if we as the weaker vessel can defeat our enemy, he is publicly showcased as a failure in front of the men. *"So let all Your enemies perish, O Lord! But let those who love Him be like the sun when it rises in its might. And the land had peace and rest for forty years* (Judges 5:31, NIV).

Arise and wake up, women of faith! Give the land peace and rest through the work of your hands. Use the talents God has given you to bring forth fruit in the land. Your fruit will be refreshing and rejuvenating for you and for others. Permit God's talents to flow through you to produce more souls and impact for the kingdom and never stop and listen to the devil's lies. He wants you to believe you are "only a woman." And yes, devil, we are women, but you know we are not frail, helpless, timid women! We are anointed women who will put our tent peg straight through your skull.

Gender, race, age, social status, or our level of education cannot determine the outcome of the fights we are engaged in. Only a faith in or lack of faith in God determines the victory or the loss in battle.

Barak, a man in Scripture, was intimated and ashamed of his position, so God used a woman to do the work instead. Barak, the man called to move forward in faith said to a woman, *"If you will go with me, I will go, but if you will not go with me, I will not go"* – (Judges 4:8, Amplified).

Deborah and Jael's ministries were innovative, and they restored and replenished God's people and areas of the earth. In the same way, God wants to partner with us in this generation. He wants us to be willing to yield to the Holy Spirit's guidance, as opposed to yielding to tradition or the philosophies of man. When we remove the spirit of religion and operate in faith and obedience, God will make a way for us to overcome the enemy forces. He will bring forth water in the desert, and He will bring dead bones back to life. And today as in the years past, we will find it can be through the hands of a woman that the enemy is defeated, if we will only believe.

If you want to step up in your ministry and your calling read this prayer out loud.

Father God, today marks a new day in my life. From this day on, I will never go backward, only forward. I won't retreat and run from my enemy- I will face him head on. I refuse to allow my gender, race, or any other human characteristic to determine my future. If You say to move forward and to perform the work, I will move forward in faith. I believe You are with me and You have called me to be the exact gender, race, and person I am. These characteristics don't disqualify me; they qualify me, for the precise mission You have given me to do. Let me never forget who I am in Christ and let me never again listen to the voice of the snake whispering lies to deter me from stomping on his head. It is in Jesus' name I pray. Amen.

4

The Mission of Snakes

Thieves steal another person's property, usually by stealth and without force, because they intend to avoid detection. Thieves want to hide and do their dirty work in the shadows, so they are not discovered. When thieves break into a person's car, home, or other personal property, using violence, it is generally because they are seen and confronted with their crime and are nervous about their punishment.

Thieves and snakes share many similar characteristics. In nature, snakes hide and often take things that do not belong to them, such as bird eggs. Snakes do not want to be discovered, especially by humans. When snakes know they are predators and not prey, they will break in and steal. But when they are confronted and challenged by a human being, who is superior to them, they often run away in fear for their lives.

Occasionally snakes feel superior to humans, especially when they sense the people are afraid of them. Many psychologists have studied human and snake relationships and assert that nearly half of the population is afraid of snakes, a phenomenon they often attribute to evolution, culture, and society. However, those of us who are Christians know the turbulent relationship with reptiles, specifically snakes. We realize the Lord caused the enmity between snakes and man.

Genesis 3:15 tells us, *"And I will put enmity (open hostility) Between you and the woman, And between your seed (offspring) and her Seed; He shall [fatally] bruise your head, And you shall [only] bruise His heel."* (AMPC)

Some people have chosen to ignore and neutralize the human and snake relationship. Some humans choose to bring these wild animals into their homes. Consider those who bring pythons, deemed to be nonvenomous and relatively docile and timid snakes, into their homes with their families. These individuals claim the snakes are not aggressive and resist confrontation, so they feel safe to welcome into the home.

However, most people agree that other breeds of snakes, such as vipers and rattlesnakes, often hold their ground and are more aggressive toward any and every human they encounter. These snakes are deadly, and even a single bite will kill or injure a human. Rattlesnakes, for instance, are said to hold enough venom to kill up to five humans, if given the opportunity in one single bite.

Likewise, the devil, often called the snake — and demons who work for him — are full of diverse spirits and potency of poison. All demon spirits do not all operate the same or hold the same power and the same amount of venom. Although all demon spirits are unclean, unholy and evil, the degree of the venom they carry is not equalized, and their behavior isn't synonymous. Evil spirits have characteristics, and some are more aggressive towards people, while others hide and attempt to be obscured, undetected by humanity.

Matthew 12:43-45 teaches, *"But when the unclean spirit has gone out of a man, it roams through dry [arid] places in search of rest, but it does not find any. Then it says, I will go back to my house from which I came out. And when it arrives, it finds the place unoccupied, swept, put in order, and decorated. Then it goes and brings with it seven other spirits more wicked than itself, and they go in and make their home there. And the last condition of that man becomes worse than the first. So also shall it be with this wicked generation."* (AMPC)

Foolish people handle snakes without spiritual protection and the oil of the Holy Spirit. The unclean spirits look for a home, and like snakes in the natural world, spiritual snakes need certain conditions to properly move and function in the spirit world. Snakes cannot move around in nature on their own. They need the sun and the warmth to heat their bodies due to their cold-blooded nature. In the spirit realm demons look for places that will allow them to move and operate. They look for people and places that allow them to live and survive, and at times even welcome them into their homes.

It is foolish to believe bringing a snake, even a seemingly harmless one, into your home is not dangerous. Many people have found out the hard way that their python, the nonaggressive, proposed "non-lethal" pet, is a murder and a thief of life. Pythons have stolen the life of many because a fool presumed, they were safe in the presence of an enemy.

Christians who are full of the Holy Spirit will have a "no tolerance" policy in their relationships with demons because we realize they are not holy or refreshing to our spirits. Born again believers crave the water. We crave the oil and the pure Spirit of life and there is a evident difference between the Holy Spirit and unholy ones. This is why discernment of spirits is a gift of the Holy Spirit. Paul writes, *"The natural person does not accept the things of the Spirit of God, for they are folly to him, and he is not able to understand them because they are spiritually discerned"* (First Corinthians 2:14, NIV).

The ability to discern the truth from a lie is a gift from God. Realizing who the enemy is and staying away from the enemy, unless we are forced to handle the intruder, is the best way to handle the demonic realm. We do not welcome evil spirits, or call for them, but when we find them, we cast them out.

The majority of homeowners do not seek out snakes. They simply find out there is one hiding or encroaching on their property. In these scenarios, the snakes need to be driven out and done away with, not ignored, because they were attempting to occupy a place that doesn't belong to them. In the same way, Christians should never ignore the devils God allows them to see, because if God reveals them to us, then He wants us to deal with them.

Many times when we are handling God's business they will manifest to try to divert and distract us from completing our mission. There is a big difference between dealing with a snake when it encroaches you and attacks you, and looking for, tolerating, and welcoming snakes into your life and your home. Paul was not looking for a snake when he encountered one after being shipwrecked on the island of Malta. He was performing his duties as a follower of Christ advancing the gospel, and the snake appeared and attempted to stop him from continuing in his work.

Acts 28:3 says, *"But when Paul had gathered a bundle of sticks and laid them on the fire, a viper crawled out because of the heat and fastened itself on his hand. When the natives saw the creature hanging from his hand, they began saying to one another, "Undoubtedly this man is a murderer, and though he has been saved from the sea, Justice [the avenging goddess] has not permitted him to live.""* (AMPC)

The natives lacked spiritual discernment. They didn't have the ability to properly discern who was working for God and who was working for the devil because they lived their lives without the Holy Spirit. If we are going to discern good and evil, and if we are going to know which spirits mean us harm and which Spirit brings us life, then we must be born again and baptized in the Holy Spirit. God gifts us with the discernment of spirits to protect us from the enemy. He allows us to see and understand all things clearly.

The snake's intended to steal Paul's ministry and credibility, and, if possible, his life. When they saw the snake attacking Paul, the people assumed he was in sin and that he was being judged for his immoral or unethical behavior. Often when the devil comes against members in the body of Christ, he wants to steal their credibility and their ministry. He wants people to see a snake bite and assume the believer is being punished by God, because when a person lacks discernment of spirits, they will fall prey to this mislabeling trap.

If the person attacked doesn't use their faith and shake off the attack of the devil, the spiritual snake can often take over their life. However, this does not have to be the narrative of the Christian, as we see through Paul's life. Christians have the ability and the authority to command the situation. They can change the script and rewrite the story. Christians can take the pen out of the 's devil's hand and put it back into the hands of God.

Acts 28:5-6 explains, *"Then Paul [simply] shook the creature off into the fire and suffered no ill effects. But they stood watching and expecting him to swell up or suddenly drop dead. But after they had waited a long time and had seen nothing unusual happen to him, they changed their minds and began saying that he was a god."* (AMPC)

One of the deadliest creatures in the world attempted to stop Paul, but because of who he was in Christ, the snake couldn't fulfill his mission. The city people knew the snake bite would have taken out anyone else, but because of his relationship to God, Paul was not harmed by the serpent. In Mark 16:18, Jesus teaches, *"They will pick up serpents, and if they drink anything deadly, it will not hurt them; they will lay hands on the sick, and they will get well."* (NIV)

Handling serpents should not be pursued, as some in the Church have assumed and wrongfully done. These scriptures are not written to teach the church to be unwise and chase after snakes and devils. However, the Church must be prepared to take them on when they manifest themselves and attempt to stop our ministries and the advancement of the kingdom of God. We must realize we are going to encounter the devil if we are truly pursuing and performing the works of God, as in the life of Paul, because the devil doesn't want us to continue in our Godly mission.

As cowards, many demons willingly run away when they are challenged. These spirits are spineless creatures, who know the power of Jesus Christ, so they are eager and willing to leave when they are challenged by the man or woman of God. Yet some spirits may hold onto their positions. These spirits act aggressively because they want to continue to poison as many people as possible. They do not want to give up their position, and they will fight harder to remain. These demons, if given the opportunity, will hold their place and refuse to move unless they are taken out by force. They require a higher level of functioning in the faith to remove.

Matthew's Gospel describes this kind of situation. Matthew 17:15-21 says, "*Lord, do pity and have mercy on my son, for he has epilepsy (is moonstruck) and he suffers terribly; for frequently he falls into the fire and many times into the water. And I brought him to Your disciples, and they were not able to cure him. And Jesus answered, O you unbelieving (warped, wayward, rebellious) and thoroughly perverse generation! How long am I to remain with you? How long am I to bear with you? Bring him here to Me. And Jesus rebuked the demon, and it came out of him, and the boy was cured instantly. Then the disciples came to Jesus and asked privately, Why could we not drive it out? He said to them, Because of the littleness of your faith [that is, your lack of firmly relying trust]. For truly I say to you, if you have faith [that is living] like a grain of mustard seed, you can say to this mountain, Move from here to yonder place, and it will move; and nothing will be impossible to you. But this kind does not go out except by prayer and fasting.*" (AMPC)

Faith must be cultivated and increased. Like working out in the gym, the first time we use our faith is going to be different from the hundredth time we use it. The demon in Matthew—17 was not too powerful to be removed, because Jesus easily removed the demon from the boy. Jesus instantly cured the boy because Jesus knew the devil was not a challenge or a threat. and He had perfect faith and trust in His authority that was given to Him by God.

Jesus Christ and God the Father are one, and when we are in Christ, we are also one with God.

John 10:30-38 says, "*I and the Father are One. Again the Jews brought up stones to stone Him. Jesus said to them, 'My Father has enabled Me to do many good deeds. [I have shown many acts of mercy in your presence.] For which of these do you mean to stone Me?' The Jews replied, 'We are not go-*

ing to stone You for a good act, but for blasphemy, because You, a mere Man, make Yourself [out to be] God.'"

Jesus answered, Is it not written in your Law, I said, You are gods? So men are called gods [by the Law], men to whom God's message came—and the Scripture cannot be set aside or cancelled or broken or annulled— [If that is true] do you say of the One Whom the Father consecrated and dedicated and set apart for Himself and sent into the world, You are blaspheming, because I said, I am the Son of God?

If I am not doing the works [performing the deeds] of My Father, then do not believe Me [do not adhere to Me and trust Me and rely on Me]. But if I do them, even though you do not believe Me or have faith in Me, [at least] believe the works and have faith in what I do, in order that you may know and understand [clearly] that the Father is in Me, and I am in the Father [One with Him]." (AMPC)

The relationship between the Church and God the Father, and Jesus Christ the Son of God, permits us to do the supernatural work of ministry. When we perform this work, we can expect nothing more than the religious leaders, and the world alike, to assume we are gods, because they can see we are operating under a supernatural force and anointing. Many people, especially the fraudulent religious leaders, hate this truth. Fraudulent religious people despise that the Lord has permitted His people to perform supernatural signs, healings, and wonders on the earth, because they themselves are not doing the work of the Father and we expose them for their deception and lies.

Moses was in one of the most wicked societies of the day. The Egyptians were full of the devil and worshiped false gods. These demons' spirits had complete control of their culture and the people's identities. Yet when Moses was living in the land, he was not overtaken by these spirits, even as a child raised in the knowledge of the demonic.

As God called Moses into ministry, one of the first things He showed Moses was that he had power and authority over the serpents/spirits, as well as over the evil people of the land — from the highest ruler to the lowest citizen.

Exodus 4:1-5 explains, *"And Moses answered, But behold, they will not believe me or listen to and obey my voice; for they will say, The Lord has not appeared to you. And the Lord said to him, What is that in your hand? And he said, A rod. And He said, Cast it on the ground. And he did so and it became a serpent [the symbol of royal and divine power worn on the crown of the Pharaohs]; and Moses fled from before it. And the Lord said to Moses, Put forth your hand and take it by the tail. And he stretched out his hand and caught it, and it became a rod in his hand, [This you shall do, said the Lord] that the elders may believe that the Lord, the God of their fathers, of Abraham, of Isaac, and of Jacob, has indeed appeared to you."* (AMPC)

As we stand boldly knowing we are in Christ we never need to fear or be intimidated. Even when it looks as though the enemy is encroaching and trying to steal from us, we can know we are the ones with the ultimate victory because, in Christ, we are in control of the earth and the creatures living on it. Moses operated in authority and power under the old covenant, and today we have an even better covenant. The worst people, the worst cultures, and the worst demons have zero right or ability to encroach and steal what the Lord has given us to do, and in faith we can command them to do what we say for them to do.

The Church will not be stopped by anyone or anything attempting to come against us in these last days. There is no weapon formed against us that will prosper. God promised us we could pick up any deadly thing, and when it tries to bite us, it will not prevail. God said the serpent is beneath us and subservient to us, both the Christian man and woman alike.

Acts 7:51-58 tells us, *"You stiff-necked people! Your hearts and ears are still uncircumcised. You are just like your ancestors: You always resist the Holy Spirit! Was there ever a prophet your ancestors did not persecute? They even killed those who predicted the coming of the Righteous One. And now you have betrayed and murdered him— you who have received the law that was given through angels but have not obeyed it.*

When the members of the Sanhedrin heard this, they were furious and gnashed their teeth at him. But Stephen, full of the Holy Spirit, looked up to heaven and saw the glory of God, and Jesus standing at the right hand of God. "Look," he said, "I see heaven open and the Son of Man standing at the right hand of God. At this they covered their ears and, yelling at the top of their voices, they all rushed at him, dragged him out of the city and began to stone him. Meanwhile, the witnesses laid their coats at the feet of a young man named Saul." (NIV)

As we see outlined in this scripture, some of the most venomous snakes are religious people. And religious leaders who carry the spirit of religion but do not carry the Holy Spirit will be judged the harshest, because they murdered people in the name of religion. Stephen was killed by religious people, as was Jesus and many of the other disciples.

Leaders and fraudulent members from the past and into the present age despise those whom God has ordained called. They hate those who are filled with His Holy Spirit. And instead of helping the mission of the Church these men and women attempt to stop and tear down the people, and the ministries ordained and established by God, all the while attesting to be a believer themselves. Yet despite the attempt to remain hidden and covert, the discerning Christian following God sees the truth. They see through the lies and deception man cannot see.

God always tells His people what the enemy is doing. He prepares the Church for the mission they are assigned to, and He will tell us the secret things that impossible to know without the help of the Holy Spirit. Second Kings 6:12 notes, *"One of his servants said, "None [of us is helping him], my lord, O king; but Elisha, the prophet who is in Israel, tells the king of Israel the words that you speak in your bedroom."* (AMPC)

God will allow His prophets to hear the secret conversations of His enemies. He will give them access into the spirit realm where nothing is hidden and everything will be revealed. As it was with Elisha, those who do evil or scheme to perpetrate evil against the Church will find themselves exposed and vulnerable, because we can see their words, deeds, and plans.

We will find devils in the world and devils in churches. We will encounter different species of snakes and different characteristics of devils, but regardless of the snake, we can pick them up and throw them out. We can cast them out and away from our life and the lives of those who want to be delivered when we are in Christ Jesus, through the authority granted to us and the power of God. Luke 10:19 says, *"Listen carefully: I have given you authority [that you now possess] to tread on serpents and scorpions, and [the ability to exercise authority] over all the power of the enemy (Satan); and nothing will [in any way] harm you."* (AMPC)

5

Bully Brothers: Jealous Family Members

In most families, there exists a mix of both healthy and unhealthy family members. Within the family, it is possible for individuals to emerge as healthy and successful despite facing setbacks and challenges. These individuals demonstrate a determination to thrive and advocate for their well-being. Pursuing health and wellness is a choice. People either want to grow and develop properly, or they choose to succumb to their problems and challenges.

Jesus Christ didn't die for our sins to keep us stuck in dysfunctional families and family patterns. His crucifixion and resurrection were intended to empower us to triumph over sin and adversity, allowing us to connect with a healthy and nurturing family system. A healthy mind, body, and spirit working in unison is God's plan for His children. First Thessalonians 5:23 explains, *"May God himself, the God of peace, sanctify you through and through. May your whole spirit, soul and body be kept blameless at the coming of our Lord Jesus Christ."* (NIV)

Sanctification, the process of being purified from sin encompasses the mind, body, and spirit part of the man. God included all three parts of the man within His healing plan. Those who are committed to obeying God and understanding His decrees will develop the ability to discern between healthy and unhealthy behaviors and thoughts. They will come to understand what it truly means to be a Christian, which distinguishes us from the broader world, beginning in their approach to health.

Outside of a relationship with Jesus Christ, people can successfully resist evil and overcome challenges in life through their human self-will and determination. However, self-will and effort can only take people so far. There are many situations in which humans need more than their own drive can offer.

Psychologists and sociologists often study people's behavior and try to alter it through natural means, but as Christians, we must acknowledge that behaviorism and positive thinking can only get humans so far. Human systems, institutions, and behaviorism can facilitate healing, restoration, and the promotion of normalcy, but only to a limited extent.

People need to be born again and washed of their sin if they are going to experience an abundant life. Numerous battles, experiences, and circumstances demand a formidable force—a supernatural Savior who advocates for us in the spiritual realm. Engaging in battle against the forces of darkness alone will ultimately yield no success; however, united with our Savior, we will achieve victory time and again.

The book of Acts chapter 19 tells us about some men who attempted to go against the forces of darkness without Jesus as their Savior. They believed they could overpower the evil spirits residing within a man by invoking the name of Jesus, despite not having a personal relationship with Him. These individuals had not experienced spiritual rebirth or received authority in the spiritual realm; as a result, they were vulnerable to being overpowered by the enemy.

"God did extraordinary miracles through Paul, so that even handkerchiefs and aprons that had touched him were taken to the sick, and their illnesses were cured and the evil spirits left them. Some Jews who went around driving out evil spirits tried to invoke the name of the Lord Jesus over those who were demon-possessed. They would say, "In the name of the Jesus whom Paul

preaches, I command you to come out." Seven sons of Sceva, a Jewish chief priest, were doing this. One day the evil spirit answered them, "Jesus I know, and Paul I know about, but who are you?" Then the man who had the evil spirit jumped on them and overpowered them all. He gave them such a beating that they ran out of the house naked and bleeding" (Acts 19:11-16, NIV).

To be within the family of Jesus, we must undergo a spiritual rebirth. Until we are transformed into new creations and we receive the baptism of the Holy Spirit, we lack the strength, health, and authority necessary to confront evil effectively. It is essential to rely on Jesus Christ and the Holy Spirit and seek divine protection in order to fully experience life and exercise our rightful leadership on earth. If we are not saved and born again, we cannot achieve completeness in our spiritual, emotional, or physical strength.

First Corinthians 10:13 says, *"For no temptation (no trial regarded as enticing to sin), [no matter how it comes or where it leads] has over taken you and laid hold on you that is not common to man [that is, no temptation or trial has come to you that is beyond human resistance and that is not adjusted and adapted and belonging to human experience, and such as man can bear]. But God is faithful [to His Word and to His compassionate nature], and He [can be trusted] not to let you be tempted and tried beyond your ability and strength of resistance and power to endure, but with the temptation He will [always] also provide the way out (the means of escape to a landing place), that you may be capable and strong and powerful to bear up under it patiently."* (AMPC)

If a storm has come into our lives, we can know we will make it through. When we are connected to Jesus, storms will come, but they can't take us out. Satan brings storms into our life because he wants to steal our faith and make us turn back from the path God has for us. When the disciples were in the boat with Jesus, they were instructed to go to the other side, but because Satan didn't want them to make it to their destination, he sent a storm.

Matthew 8:23-26 tells us, *"And after He got into the boat, His disciples followed Him. And suddenly, behold, there arose a violent storm on the sea, so that the boat was being covered up by the waves; but He was sleeping. And they went and awakened Him saying, Lord, rescue and preserve us! We are perishing! And He said to them, Why are you timid and afraid, O you of little faith? Then He got up and rebuked the winds and the sea, and there was a great and wonderful calm (a perfect peaceableness)."* (NIV)

Jesus wants us to rest in the assurance of our protection. He wants us to use our faith through His name to rebuke the storms in our life. As Christ's followers, the enemy couldn't sink their ship. He did not have the strength and power to make their ship go down. Yet, the devil is a bully, one who works to scare and intimidate anyone who presents themselves as spiritually weak and vulnerable. He will take as much as possible, but the good news is he can only take what we give him. Cowering in fear and refusing to confront the enemy allows him to have the influence he wants in our lives.

Satan knows when we stand firm in faith, acknowledging and rebuking him, he must flee. Jesus rebuked the storm because it wasn't sent from God, and it had no right to be there. The fear, the storm, and the setback were an attempt to get the men to turn back and run in fear from their future and their God given destination.

Second Timothy 1:7 explains, *"For God did not give us a spirit of timidity (of cowardice, of craven and cringing and fawning fear), but [He has given us a spirit] of power and of love and of calm and well-balanced mind and discipline and self-control."* (AMPC)

Satan mission is to keep Christians from reaching their destination given to them by God. He wants to stop us from progressing, growing, and prospering because he knows God is going to work with us in a mighty way to destroy him. Satan mainly works through the emotional and physical senses. He wants people to look at their external surroundings and use them as their guide.

To operate in our authority and show strength in our mind, emotions, and our bodies, we must learn to subdue our thoughts and take them captive. We must operate on a higher level, the spiritual level, ignoring what we think, see, and feel, and relying fully on God.

Isaiah 11:2-3 tells us, *"And the Spirit of the Lord shall rest upon Him—the Spirit of wisdom and understanding, the Spirit of counsel and might, the Spirit of knowledge and of the reverential and obedient fear of the Lord—And shall make Him of quick understanding, and His delight shall be in the reverential and obedient fear of the Lord. And He shall not judge by the sight of His eyes, neither decide by the hearing of His ears;"* (AMPC)

Satan's plan is to convince people to question the power and the help they have within the spiritual realm so he can take over the reins of their lives. Human submission and conformity are the methods that evil spirits attain power and strength. Without human cooperation, the devil must stop his work. If people resist relying on their own strength, and they rebuke the spirit of fear or any other unclean spirit encroaching on our lives, then they will silence it and take control of the situation.

Evil spirits are after the anointing, and they know when people give way to evil, they can lose their protection from God. When King David gave into temptation, he faced defeat by Satan in one of his battles with him. This outcome angered God, as David was not meant to lose a fight. As an heir to salvation and a partner with God, he possessed the strength and authority to overcome all temptations. He had the capability to resist the evil one, but he succumbed to the weaknesses of the flesh and human reasoning.

Second Samuel 12:7-12 explains,

"Then Nathan said to David, "You are that man! The Lord, the God of Israel, says: I anointed you king of Israel and saved you from the power of Saul. I gave you your master's house and his wives and the kingdoms of Israel and Judah. And if that had not been enough, I would have given you much, much more. Why, then, have you despised the word of the Lord and done this horrible deed? For you have murdered Uriah the Hittite with the sword of the Ammonites and stolen his wife. From this time on, your family will live by the sword because you have despised me by taking Uriah's wife to be your own. "This is what the Lord says: Because of what you have done, I will cause your own household to rebel against you. I will give your wives to

another man before your very eyes, and he will go to bed with them in public view. You did it secretly, but I will make this happen to you openly in the sight of all Israel."'" (NIV)

God forgave David and continued to work through him, blessing him and using him powerfully. However, David faced consequences for his sins and was held accountable for his compromises with temptation and evil. *Second Samuel 12: 13-14 explains, "Then David confessed to Nathan, "I have sinned against the Lord." Nathan replied, "Yes, but the Lord has forgiven you, and you won't die for this sin. Nevertheless, because you have shown utter contempt for the word of the Lord by doing this, your child will die."'"* (NIV)

Evil spirits need a host because they do not have physical bodies. Satan's dirty work is done using human beings who are ignorant or indifferent about his influence in their lives and choices.

By willingly yielding to Satan and sin, people become whores for the devil, and he is their pimp. Satan will use and abuse the bodies of the man and the woman permitting him access to their souls and lives. Satan often tempts, lures, and tricks people into sin by making the sin look enticing, fun, or enjoyable. He promises prosperity, happiness, and protection. But once people bite the apple, they realize they have brought death into their lives, and then it is too late.

Consider Moses, who recognized the allure of pleasure and ease yet chose to resist it in pursuit of spiritual strength. He was aware of Satan's strategy to present offerings that seem beneficial to the flesh. Hebrews 11:25-26 says, *"Because he preferred to share the oppression [suffer the hardships] and bear the shame of the people of God rather than to have the fleeting enjoyment of a sinful life. He considered the contempt and abuse and shame [borne for] the Christ (the Messiah Who was to come) to be greater wealth than all the treasures of Egypt, for he looked forward and away to the reward (recompense)."* (AMPC)

Satan can offer people riches, positions, and things on the earth. As Satan tempted Jesus *"he said to Him, "All these things I will give You, if You fall down and worship me"* (Matthew 4:9, NIV). Satan does have power when people yield to him. Being successful, rich, and evil is possible, but in these demonically inspired and given positions, people are being violated and used by a spirit that hates them. Even when Satan appears to be helpful or caring, his true colors of an abuser and trafficker will eventually be revealed.

What Satan doesn't want us to know is that serving the Lord leads to greater riches and blessings than he can offer. God doesn't use us; He helps us and partners with us to improve our lives. Satan is looking for what he can get from us, but God is looking for what He can give us. Proverbs 10:22 tells us, *"The blessing of the Lord brings [true] riches, And He adds no sorrow to it [for it comes as a blessing from God]." (AMPC).*

In this last period before Christ returns, Christians will become prosperous and powerful on the earth, and our blessings will not bring forth sorrow. Men and women who are rich and successful because of the blessing and the anointing of God will soar like eagles. They will not be weary, or tired. Isaiah 40:31 says, *"But those who wait for the LORD [who expect, look for, and hope in Him] Will gain new strength and renew their power; They will lift up their wings [and rise up close to God] like eagles [rising toward the sun]; They will run and not become weary, They will walk and not grow tired." (AMPC)*

As we stay in tune with God and His plan for our lives, we will always end up better off than before. We will always go forward, not backwards. God has good plans for us. He is going to lead us to still waters. Proverbs 4:18 tells us, *"But the path of the just (righteous) is like the light of dawn, That shines brighter and brighter until [it reaches its full strength and glory in] the perfect day." (AMPC)*

We mentioned the story of Esther in an earlier chapter. In it, Haman, who worked for the king, appeared to be prosperous and successful. He was living in the palace with the king, and he had a high-ranking, noble position in the king's house. But Haman was evil and worked for the devil. His prosperity and position were fragile, and they were taken from him in an instant. Haman's life didn't finish well because he was killed. He didn't get to enjoy anything he had worked for.

Having a powerful position, being a leader on the earth, or having money and fame doesn't mean a person pleases God. Oftentimes Satan gives evil people positions so he can use them to do his dirty work. In many mob families, the boss would assign younger ranking people to do the work they didn't want to do. They would put the lives of the youngsters on the line so they could sit back and enjoy the work done on their behalf.

Satan is like a corrupt mob boss. He is a gang leader who has no love for anyone. He uses and takes from whomever and whatever will give him what he desires. There is no loyalty. There is no bond. When he finishes with the people who work for him, they may be dead or barely hanging on, but he doesn't care as long as they have done the job he had for them.

Esther 3:1-5 contrasts two men with two different missions and two different masters. Mordecai was a godly man, a man of faith and purpose. He was a man who was honest, and loyal to the king he served. He cared about the lives of others. He was a helper to his people. Conversely, Haman was a self-serving wicked man. He had no loyalty to his king, his duty, or his position, or even to his own soul. He chased death, murder, and evil. He was willing to take out anyone who wouldn't do what he wanted them to do using any means possible.

We can see how Haman deteriorated.

"After these events King Ahasuerus promoted Haman, son of Hamme-datha the Agagite, to high rank, seating him above all his fellow officials. All the king's servants who were at the royal gate would kneel and bow down to Haman, for that is what the king had ordered in his regard. Mordecai, how-ever, would not kneel and bow down. The king's servants who were at the royal gate said to Mordecai, "Why do you disobey the king's order?" When they had reminded him day after day and he would not listen to them, they informed Haman, to see whether Mordecai's explanation would prevail, since he had told them that he was a Jew. When Haman observed that Mordecai

would not kneel and bow down to him, he was filled with anger" (Esther 3:1-5, New Living).

Satan humiliates and steals a man or a woman's identity and their purpose. He steals God's beautiful creation and demeans and degrades it through evil works and deeds until there is nothing left of the man. Conversely, God made us for connection, love, and acceptance. God sees us for who we are and who we are supposed to be, and He does anything in His power to help build us up and take us to a higher level than we were before.

In sports, a good coach will inspire their players to rise and thrive in the game. They will challenge the players, but they challenge them to strengthen them and empower them for success. Loving coaches know they don't own the player, but they attach themselves to the player to help them become the best version of themselves. God is the good coach. He is our Father who wants us to be strong, healthy, and successful.

Matthew 7:9-11 explains, *"You parents—if your children ask for a loaf of bread, do you give them a stone instead? Or if they ask for a fish, do you give them a snake? Of course not! So if you sinful people know how to give good gifts to your children, how much more will your heavenly Father give good gifts to those who ask him."* (NLT)

God has good gifts for us. He has plans to give us a life of dignity and glory. A healthy and strong father is proud of his children because they represent him. Both God's and Satan's fatherhood mark will be left on humanity. Children of God resemble Him, and children of Satan look and act like him. Jesus knew this truth well: *Then the Pharisees said to Him, "Where is this Father of Yours?" Jesus answered, "You know neither Me nor My Father; if you knew Me, you would know My Father also"* (John 8:19, Amplified).

God wants us to prosper because when we prosper, we represent Him. Jesus represented the Father in heaven during His time on the earth. He showed the world who God is and what God wanted. A child who commits crimes brings shame on their mother and father.

The parents share in shame and the community's rejection. Likewise, when a child is kind, healthy, and strong, the parents receive glory and recognition for their child's behavior.

Christians are going to assume high positions and places of influence and authority in this last hour of time. We are going to change neighborhoods, communities, cities, and the nations we live in. We have the Father's blessing and resources to do this. We have the tools and the weapons to perform the work He wants us to do. This is the last season of time. Now is the time to harvest and work the fields for the Lord. *"Then I will give you your rains in their season, and the land shall yield its increase, and the trees of the field shall yield their fruit"* (Leviticus 26:4, Amplified).

However we must stand firm in our positions remaining fully convinced of what God has given us so it cannot be stolen by our enemy. Mordecai refused to bow down to evil. He stood strong in his position and his authority as a believer, and this stance and conviction was the key to finding blessing and favor with the Lord.

For Mordecai he needed to represent God to the ungodly people of the king's staff showing us that we will need to represent God to the ungodly. However there are times when we will be asked to take the same position and stand within the household of faith. In these circumstances, we must be proud of the blessing and wear the rainbow coat telling the world who our father is even if our brothers don't like it.

In Scripture, Joseph knew he had a place of influence on the earth. He knew the blessing was on his life, because he was born into a family of promise. Joseph remained unconcerned about his brothers, directing his attention toward God, which shielded him from the evil influences surrounding him. He recognized his divine love and purpose, understanding that he would be utilized by God during the specific season of his life. In contrast, his brothers fixated on worldly matters, which ultimately constrained their ability to fully receive their blessings.

David, like Joseph's brothers, wanted to stop him from reaching his destiny because they were jealous of him. Their focus was on people and natural wisdom, not God. Both set of brothers compared themselves to others, instead of owning their unique identity and purpose for God. As Paul says, *"Not that we [have the audacity to] venture to class or [even to] compare ourselves with some who exalt and furnish testimonials for themselves! However, when they measure themselves with themselves and compare themselves with one another, they are without understanding and behave unwisely"* (2 Corinthians 10:12, Amplified).

Neither jealously or hatred from the world or from our brothers can stop us from getting what God has for us. Because no person or devil has the power to prevent us from receiving the blessings of God. As the Doxology says, *"Praise God from who all blessings flow."*

Genesis 37:4-11 explains, *"But when his brothers saw that their father loved [Joseph] more than all of his brothers, they hated him and could not say, Peace [in friendly greeting] to him or speak peaceably to him. Now Joseph had a dream and he told it to his brothers, and they hated him still more. And he said to them, Listen now and hear, I pray you, this dream that I have dreamed: We [brothers] were binding sheaves in the field, and behold, my sheaf arose and stood upright, and behold, your sheaves stood round about my sheaf and bowed down! His brothers said to him, Shall you indeed reign over us? Or are you going to have us as your subjects and dominate us? And they hated him all the more for his dreams and for what he said. But Joseph dreamed yet another dream and told it to his brothers [also]. He said, See here, I have dreamed again, and behold, [this time not only] eleven stars [but also] the sun and the moon bowed down and did reverence to me! And he told it to his father [as well as] his brethren. But his father rebuked him and said to him, What is the meaning of this dream that you have dreamed? Shall I and your mother and your brothers actually come to bow down ourselves to the earth and do homage to you? Joseph's brothers envied him and were jealous of him, but his father observed the saying and pondered over it."* (AMPC)

6

Religious Demons & False Prophecy

Wise people investigate to determine the origins of information they receive. One method of receiving information is through other humans, as people can be used by God or by Satan to transmit messages. Not every message we hear should be trusted. Every form of communication has an origination place. This place is important because human spokesmen may be speaking for God, or they may be speaking for our enemy.

An origin is the place a thing has begun or was created or derived from. Hearing a word without determining its origin opens the door to intercepting the demonic realm and can simultaneously limit us from receiving a word from the Lord. All believers need to discover the spirit behind the words they receive. If we want to be protected from the lies of the enemy, and hear the voice of God, we need to always seek out the origin of a thing so we can discern people, doctrines, words, and situations.

First John 4:1-6 says, *"Beloved, do not believe every spirit [speaking through a self-proclaimed prophet]; instead test the spirits to see whether they are from God, because many false prophets and teachers have gone out into the world. By this you know and recognize the Spirit of God: every spirit that acknowledges and confesses [the fact] that Jesus Christ has [actually] come in the flesh [as a man] is from God [God is its source];*

and every spirit that does not confess Jesus [acknowledging that He has come in the flesh, but would deny any of the Son's true nature] is not of God; this is the spirit of the antichrist, which you have heard is coming, and is now already in the world. Little children (believers, dear ones), you are of God and you belong to Him and have [already] overcome them [the agents of the antichrist]; because He who is in you is greater than he (Satan) who is in the world [of sinful mankind].

They [who teach twisted doctrine] are of the world and belong to it; therefore they speak from the [viewpoint of the] world [with its immoral freedom and baseless theories—demanding compliance with their opinions and ridiculing the values of the upright], and the [gullible one of the] world listens closely and pays attention to them.

We [who teach God's word] are from God [energized by the Holy Spirit], and whoever knows God [through personal experience] listens to us [and has a deeper understanding of Him]. Whoever is not of God does not listen to us. By this we know [without any doubt] the spirit of truth [motivated by God] and the spirit of error [motivated by Satan]." (AMPC)

At the micro level, the small interactions between us to the large level of macro interactions, our source of information is life-changing. Books, movies, music, and other forms of media speak to large groups of people and convey messages. These messages originate from either God or Satan. Words particularly hold power, especially when they are sung, and they can modify a trajectory of a life.

Demonically inspired messages will lead hearers into a place of bondage and blindness. The Bible is a book of light, and God's Word, either in oral or written form, permits us to see and hear clearly so we can make choices leading to life. Achieving spiritual things isn't by accident, and if we are irresponsible regarding our lives, we will never experience the abundant life God has for us. Listening to the wrong people, doctrines, or sounds, is harmful to the soul.

To change our circumstances, we need to be accountable for our time and choices. We have simple choices, such as whether to eat breakfast or not, and bigger choices of who we marry and where we live. Such choices can and do affect our bodies and our lives.

God gave us everything we need to live healthy, successful, and victorious lives in Christ. As the High Priest, Jesus has prepared us for a life of prosperity. He continually provides us with the oil we need and keeps us from living a dry life. But to be refreshed, we must be thirsty and willing to get closer to Jesus regularly, because this choice is the most important choice we can make. *"For I will pour water on the thirsty land, and streams on the dry ground; I will pour out my Spirit on your offspring, and my blessing on your descendants"* (Isaiah 44:3, NIV).

Our choices impact us and they impact others. We do not navigate our lives devoid of personal or social responsibility. The Bible affirms that our actions contribute to a greater narrative and a broader purpose. What we choose to do—or refrain from doing—holds significance not only for us but also for those around us.

Jesus coordinates a strategic plan, and He has what each person in the kingdom needs every day. God's provisions never run out. There is more than enough within the anointing of God. If we have failed to receive the things we need from God, we either don't need them, or we haven't done what we need to do to get them from Him.

In ourselves, outside of Christ we would struggle and toil like the rest of the world underneath the curse. But in Christ, we don't need to struggle anymore. In Christ, we can feed five thousand people with a little boy's lunch.

Jesus is our commander in chief. In our human military, the locations of battle and stations are coordinated, and soldiers go where they are told, instead of personally determining where they want to be. Likewise, God gives each of His soldiers an occupation, a location, and a ranking. He gives us a command and an assignment we need to fulfill to advance His kingdom. We will find everything we need to get the work done when we are on our assignment, doing what we have been told to do.

Christians who do well on their assignments will be given more, but if they fail to do a job they have been given, it will be taken and given to someone else. God will partner with whoever is willing and available to do His work.

"But ask the beasts, and they will teach you; the birds of the heavens, and they will tell you; or the bushes of the earth, and they will teach you; and the fish of the sea will declare to you. Who among all these does not know that the hand of the Lord has done this? In his hand is the life of every living thing and the breath of all mankind" (Job 12:7-10, NIV).

God invites us to partner with Him; and, if we are chosen to undertake His work, we should rejoice and express gratitude for this privilege. God has the power to raise anyone, even a stone, to fulfill His purposes and mission. He does not depend on human traditions or understanding. All of us—whether we are men, women, or children—are not selected based on our biological lineage or their social acceptability, we are selected for our commitment and love for God and His mission.

Some false teachers create children/people who agree with their false beliefs. Self-appointed preachers, teachers, or other leaders without the anointing will lead the younger or the inexperienced into sin and folly. Jesus had strong words for these deceivers: *Woe to you, teachers of the law and Pharisees, you hypocrites! You travel over land and sea to win a single convert, and when you have succeeded, you make them twice as much a child of hell as you are"* (Matthew 23:15, Amplified).

It is possible to do the work of the Lord improperly. Not everyone who identifies as a Christian embodies the faith. In fact, numerous leaders within churches globally are themselves under a curse, as they fail to engage in the works of the Lord with sincerity and integrity.

Doctrines that group people based on skin color, gender identity, financial standing, or biological association are demonic. Throughout history, deceived religious leaders have made rules about the selection process of saints. These people have consistently hated the Lord's plan to deliver people they deemed as unfit, unworthy people. Today, we see this spirit operating within many churches and places of worship, because religious demon spirits still have the same mission or assignment from their leader Satan, just in a different time period.

Any leader who welcomes or consents to demonic spirits and permits them to influence others is accountable. A failure to discern and properly perform the work of God in the temples and houses of worship is detestable and is being judged by the Lord. God is watching to see who is willing to do His work, with or without the approval of other men. And He is watching to see who works to be seen by men, with no regard to God.

"Everything they do is done for people to see: They make their phylacteries wide and the tassels on their garments long; they love the place of honor at banquets and the most important seats in the synagogues; they love to be greeted with respect in the marketplaces and to be called 'Rabbi' by others" (Matthew 23:5-7, NIV).

Being a part of a certain denomination, or other social group, isn't what saves us. We alone stand before God and are judged for our love and commitment to God. Nicodemus, a religious leader and Pharisee, went to Jesus privately to determine the truth. Even when others within his religious group believed Jesus was not doing the works of God, Nicodemus took personal responsibility for finding out the truth.

John 3:1-2 says, *"Now there was a Pharisee, a man named Nicodemus who was a member of the Jewish ruling council. He came to Jesus at night and said, "Rabbi, we know that you are a teacher who has come from God. For no one could perform the signs you are doing if God were not with him."* (NIV)

People learn from their leaders, and leaders who improperly transmit the message from God to the people rob them. New coverts to Christianity need time to develop. They need to be taught the raw truth of God's Word and in its entirety. Like a bad parent can set children down the wrong path, a bad spiritual leader can corrupt the mind of the convert. They can teach them false doctrines and lies and spoil their future.

Jesus grieved over this. He said in Matthew 23:37, *"Jerusalem, Jerusalem, you who kill the prophets and stone those sent to you, how often I have longed to gather your children together, as a hen gathers her chicks under her wings, and you were not willing."* (NIV)

The Lord establishes positions of leadership and authority. He gives us spiritual mothers and fathers. And although ultimately all people are individually responsible for their own actions of faith or disobedience, we must acknowledge the power we have as Christians. We can change lives for good or for evil. We can use the gospel as a tool to harm or to build up the people God places around us.

As we grow up in Christ and become accustomed to walking with God, we will hear His voice and instruction and identify it as the voice of truth, even when those around us choose to follow a different voice. *My sheep hear my voice, and I know them, and they follow me* (John 10:27, NIV). However in the beginning, children (new converts) will need help to learn right doctrine and wrong doctrine. New believers need the help of their spiritual leaders as a newborn baby and young child needs the protection and guidance of their parents!

As we mature in our faith, we realize we can't rely on another man's or woman's words to determine our lives. All children reach an age of accountability where they must separate from their parents and take personal responsibility for their lives. Likewise, in our faith, we all reach a point where we are no longer blameless for irresponsible actions or ignorance. At some point, we become the ones God expects to decipher the truth from a lie.

A ten-year-old who is negatively impacted by their parents is understandable. A sixty-year-old man still blaming his parents for his life is terribly wrong. All leaders need to prepare their spiritual children to launch into the world. The job of being a leader is building up an army of believers who are strong and healthy and will contribute as members of the Church. At first, we rely on our spiritual leaders significantly, but over time we learn to function on our own and take responsibility for our own lives and begin bearing spiritual children of our own.

Adulthood doesn't automatically bring forth wisdom, because wisdom must be attained through proper leadership and a younger yearning heart. Solomon became king as a child. He knew he needed help to make good decisions, so He asked God to teach him about the truth and help him to become a wise and honorable king. Solomon benefited from the guidance of a wise spiritual father, David, and actively sought counsel from God. As a result, he possessed greater wisdom than many of the older men in his vicinity, despite his youth.

Achieving wisdom requires both God and good spiritual guidance from older believers. God tells us to follow Him and He tells us to imitate and copy those who have already received the promises. Hebrews 6:12 explains, *"so that you will not be [spiritually] sluggish, but [will instead be] imitators of those who through faith [lean on God with absolute trust and confidence in Him and in His power] and by patient endurance [even when suffering] are [now] inheriting the promises."* (AMPC)

Paul explained to the Church that all our decisions have eternal consequences. *"For we [believers will be called to account and] must all appear before the judgment seat of Christ, so that each one may be repaid for what has been done in the body, whether good or bad [that is, each will be held responsible for his actions, purposes, goals, motives—the use or misuse of his time, opportunities and abilities]"* (Second Corinthians 5:10, Amplified).

Teaching incorrect doctrines from demon entities is proof that a person is under the curse and a judgment. These men are not truly born again and as fraudulent leaders they will be held responsible for their deeds because being taught the wrong thing is more detrimental than being taught nothing at all. Consider a child who is taught to lie, steal, and cheat by their parents. As children, they learn to interact with the world in an immoral way, so when they become older, they usually believe the way they have been acting is correct, even when it isn't.

Church leaders who train new coverts in false doctrines and ways of interacting with God and the world are similar to unhealthy parents. They propagate misleading teachings that foster corruption and rebellion against the truth. Consequently, their spiritual followers frequently remain entrenched in these misguided paths throughout their Christian journey. All the while, they believe they are acting appropriately, inadvertently training new converts in corrupt practices.

God gives us people to watch over spiritually. He permits us to guide certain groups. In Ezekiel, God tells Ezekiel to speak to "his" people. God wasn't saying that Ezekiel owned the people like cattle, but He was telling him to care for them as his spiritual children, children who needed to be corrected and guided into all truth.

"And the word of the Lord came to me, saying, Son of man, speak to your people [the Israelite captives in Babylon] and say to them, When I bring the sword upon a land and the people of the land take a man from among them and make him their watchman, If when he sees the sword coming upon the land, he blows the trumpet and warns the people, Then whoever hears the sound of the trumpet and does not take warning, and the sword comes and takes him away, his blood shall be upon his own head. He heard the sound of the trumpet and did not take warning; his blood shall be upon himself. But he who takes warning shall save his life. But if the watchman sees the sword coming and does not blow the trumpet and the people are not warned, and the sword comes and takes any one of them, he is taken away in and for his perversity and iniquity, but his blood will I require at the watchman's hand. So you, son of man, I have made you a watchman for the house of Israel; therefore hear the word at My mouth and give them warning from Me" (Ezekiel 33:1-7, NIV).

Many leaders have been rebuked for failing to properly care for those God has entrusted to them, as a life of personal satisfaction and ease is a life easily thwarted by Satan. Children, both physical and spiritual, need to be taught to not give into the easy path in life. It is imperative that individuals are taught to uphold what is righteous and true. They must learn from their elders the values of hard work and accountability, both to one another and to a higher moral standard. This embodies the essence of the pure gospel: a gospel rooted in diligence and a steadfast commitment to holiness and truth.

These leaders are different than the fraudulent leader; as genuine Christian leaders are trying to follow the Lord but they have made mistakes- as David and Moses both did. When God rebukes His children it is to help them to grow and continue to develop. Edification and correction from God aimed at His children is distinct from the punishment awaiting those who go out of their way to rebel God's Word attempting to change it or distort it.

Christians will undergo the Bema judgment, where their actions will be assessed by Jesus in order to receive appropriate rewards. In contrast, unbelievers and wicked leaders will not participate in the Bema judgment; as they will face condemnation to hell and be judged specifically for their evil actions and deeds, rather than any good they may have done. As God corrected David, he assured him he wouldn't die, (eternal judgment), but he did still correct and redirect him into proper leadership and truth.

In every area of life, from tithing to refraining from sexual sin, the Holy Spirit will work through leaders willing to convict and confront wrong behavior. Like a parent who disciplines their child, a good spiritual parent will train through teaching and correcting. If a church leader does not confront wrong behavior, the child will likely be spoiled and become an unproductive member of the family of God.

Through confrontation people are given a choice to learn and change. Leaders are commanded by God to warn people, both within and outside of the Church. We are obligated to tell the truth of God's Word and His laws, or we will be responsible for the failure to report the message. Our words and actions matter. We are training people for good or for evil in everything we do and say as Christians.

Our actions and our words transmit messages. They send out frequencies for the enemy or for God. Spirits direct and orchestrate people's lives, and they utilize us as a medium to implement their plans and objectives, much like a film director relies on actors to bring their vision to life.

A failure to learn proper accountability has caused many people in our American society to feel it is someone elses' responsibility when life doesn't go their way. But God's message remains the same. Choices and consequences, sowing and reaping, are God's system. Time or age doesn't bring positive change or blessing within our lives. Life isn't about chance or luck. Life is about attaining wisdom and sticking to the path of life.

God has written a script for His people's lives. He has a plan for us and a certain way we should speak and behave. When we act in accordance with His plan and script we will find we are acting out and speaking the truth. Yet when people adopt incorrect doctrine and follow unholy or corrupted leaders, they will act in accordance with Satan's agenda, all while believing they remain aligned with God's guidance and purpose.

God is a perfect parent and intends for us to be trained into righteousness and truth. A failure to do this on behalf of the leaders bothers God because He wants those children to be cared for properly, as we do for children living in the physical world. It is sad when a child's potential and life are thwarted because of the bad decisions of their leaders and parents. But when God established leadership, He allowed leaders to choose how they steward and care for their flock.

Poor parenting and leadership within the Church are comparable to unhealthy parenting in the world. Today it is commonplace to teach people God is okay to lead lifestyles of sin, such as homosexuality or free sex within the church. But like a parent who fails to do their job to their children, unhealthy leaders in the church breed sickness and disease upon the congregants. The members and children of the church under poor spiritual parents will be unwell due to being taught unhealthy spiritual doctrines.

Those of us who have attained sound doctrine and are healthy, functioning members, must stand unashamed of the truth. Doing so permits unhealthy church members to see and experience a different reality from the one in which they were raised and are a part of. Children in emotionally, physically, or spiritually sick homes will suffer, including spiritual children.

When we take a stand for righteousness and truth, we allow God to heal those who want healing. The only thing that can set people free is the truth of God's Word, and without His truth, they will continue to be sick. John 8:31-32 explains, *"So Jesus said to the Jews who had believed him, "If you abide in my word, you are truly my disciples, and you will know the truth, and the truth will set you free.""* (NIV)

Without a man or woman willing to arise and operate in God's truth, even God's people will suffer. Without an anointed man or woman of God, people are left in captivity and are not prepared in knowing how to get out of their captivity and suffering. God used Moses to deliver His people from their bondage, and without Moses, even God's people would have remained stuck in a place they were not intended to be.

Isaiah 5:13 teaches, *"Therefore My people go into captivity [to their enemies] without knowing it and because they have no knowledge [of God]. And their honorable men [their glory] are famished, and their common people are parched with thirst."* (AMPC)

God has compassion on His people who are lacking a full understanding or misunderstanding the Scriptures. But He does not have the same compassion towards the wicked people have been warned and given opportunities to change and obey the Lord, but they choose to continue in their sin and rebellion; the people who hate God and His Word, and willfully go against the commands of God because they hate the truth.

We see examples of such people in the Bible. Men like Pharaoh in Exodus and women like Jezebel in First and Second Kings, were confronted with the truth but didn't care about it. In Jesus' ministry on the earth, the Pharisees also knew the Scriptures and the truth, but they refused to accept or acknowledge it because they hated the truth of God's Word. Wicked men and women have knowledge. Though they know the truth, they hate it they have been given.

In these last days, we will see signs of corruption from people pretending to be a part of the Church. Just as the season of spring brings with it signals of its arrival, so will the remaining hour before Christ returns bring signs of His arrival. One of the signs will be the increase in false doctrines and the promotion of lawlessness, even from the pulpits and the sanctuaries attesting outwardly to being holy.

It is more important than ever to determine the origins of the messages in the world. As the Church of Jesus Christ, we must be diligent, awake, and on guard to all messages being sent, so we can assure we are receiving and teaching pure knowledge.

Jesus teaches in Matthew 24:10-13, *"At that time many will be offended and repelled [by their association with Me] and will fall away [from the One whom they should trust] and will betray one another [handing over believers to their persecutors] and will hate one another. Many false prophets will appear and mislead many. Because lawlessness is increased, the love of most people will grow cold. But the one who endures and bears up [under suffering] to the end will be saved."* (AMPC)

When we are in Christ we are married to Him. Healthy married couples operate as one team, and when they make decisions, they make them in unison. A husband and a wife who do not agree when making decisions will find trouble and conflict because God designed the woman and the man to operate in peace and oneness of heart and mind.

In the days of Noah, the women of the earth chose to join themselves to devils, who are fallen angels, and they began to marry the devils and they led them away from the Lord. As God saw the women married to the fallen angels on the earth, He was sorry He had made humanity. The mixing of evil with humanity is the reason God flooded the earth and destroyed all His creation.

Yet, amid the corruption, Noah had chosen to remain faithful and committed to God and His faithfulness. Noah was spared from the devastation and the judgment of the all-consuming flood, because he heard and responded to the Lord's messages! And Noah did not enter the ark alone. He took those under his leadership with him.

Genesis 6:1-8 says, *"When human beings began to increase in number on the earth and daughters were born to them, the sons of God saw that the daughters of humans were beautiful, and they married any of them they chose. Then the Lord said, "My Spirit will not contend with humans forever, for they are mortal; their days will be a hundred and twenty years." The Nephilim were on the earth in those days—and also afterward—when the sons of God went to the daughters of humans and had children by them. They were the heroes of old, men of renown. The Lord saw how great the wickedness of the human race had become on the earth, and that every inclination of the thoughts of the human heart was only evil all the time. The Lord regretted that he had made human beings on the earth, and his heart was deeply troubled. So the Lord said, "I will wipe from the face of the earth the human race I have created—and with them the animals, the birds and the creatures that move along the ground—for I regret that I have made them." But Noah found favor in the eyes of the Lord."* (NIV)

Some men and women of the world willingly give themselves over to demons allowing demons to determine their words and actions. Instead of being yoked with the Father, these men and women permit the trajectory of their life to be one of destruction and damnation. But they are not settled to go alone. They want to take converts and undiscerning people with them if they can. They want to conceive and birth demonic children taking those children to hell- as Noah took his children to salvation.

In Matthew 24:37 Jesus instructs us, *"For the coming of the Son of Man (the Messiah) will be just like the days of Noah. For as in those days before the flood they were eating and drinking, marrying and giving in marriage, until the [very] day when Noah entered the ark,"* (AMPC)

Contamination through unfaithfulness is the devil's method of corrupting and turning the hearts of women and men from the Lord. If Satan can contaminate people within the Church, he knows he can breed sickness, disease, and sin there. First Corinthians 15:58 says, *"Therefore, my beloved brothers and sisters, be steadfast, immovable, always excelling in the work of the Lord [always doing your best and doing more than is needed], being continually aware that your labor [even to the point of exhaustion] in the Lord is not futile nor wasted [it is never without purpose]."* (AMPC)

God is a holy and jealous God. When we accept Jesus Christ as our Savior, we are pledging to be faithful to Him and Him alone. Whores and unfaithful men and women are not going to be given a place in the house of God if they do not repent and turn from their deeds. Sexual immorality in human and spiritual relationships is strictly forbid den. First Corinthians 10:21 explains, "You cannot drink [both] the Lord's cup and the cup of demons. You cannot share in both the Lord's table and the table of demons [thereby becoming partners with them]." (AMPC)

Adam and Eve blamed each other for sin, but God held them both accountable, and they were given a separate and individualized punishment. When Ananias sand Sapphira were caught in sin, the Holy Spirit let them give an account for their behavior separately. They were both given a chance to be honest. Likewise, God will always give us opportunities to accept Him or deny Him. And when we are presented with good versus evil, honesty versus lying, we must choose for ourselves, and what we choose is witnessed by and will be remembered by God.

Acts 5:1-11 teaches, *"But then a man named Ananias, with the consent of his wife Sapphira, sold some property. With his wife's full knowledge, he kept back some of the money for himself and brought the remainder and laid it at the apostles' feet. Peter asked, "Ananias, why has Satan filled your heart so that you should lie to the Holy Spirit and keep back some of the money you got for the land? As long as it remained unsold, wasn't it your own? And after it was sold, wasn't the money at your disposal? So how could you have thought of doing what you did? You didn't lie only to men, but also to God!"*

When Ananias heard these words, he fell down and died. And great fear seized everyone who heard about it. The young men got up, wrapped him up, carried him outside, and buried him. After an interval of about three hours, Ananias' wife came in, not knowing what had happened. So Peter asked her, "Tell me, did you sell the land for that price?" She answered, "Yes, that was the price."

"How could you have agreed together to test the Spirit of the Lord?" Peter asked her. "Listen! The feet of the men who buried your husband are at the door, and these men will carry you outside as well." She instantly fell down at Peter's feet and died. When the young men came in, they found her dead. So they carried her out and buried her next to her husband. And great fear seized the whole church and everyone else who heard about this." (NIV)

Ananias and Sapphira were obligated to operate in unison and in truth towards their church family as commanded by God. Yet, they conspired to deceive the Holy Spirit, and their fellow brethren, despite being given the opportunity to repent and confess their wrongdoing. Ultimately, both chose to persist in their deception, remaining aligned with the demonic realm. Consequently, God judged them for their decision showing us that our actions towards others in the Church of Jesus Christ are monitored and recorded.

Ananias and Sapphira were married. However, the Scriptures teach us even married couples are to be held individually responsible for their behavior and their choices. If one of the two in the marriage had been willing to come forward, admitting their sin, the Lord would have permitted them to live. God isn't a socialist. God allows for each of us to give an account for our own life and choices, both the good and the bad. *So then, each of us will give an account of himself to God* (Romans 14:12, NIV).

Heaven has a phenomenal record keeping system. God takes note of the behavior and the choices of the people living on the earth. The unsaved people will be judged for their sins, and the saved will be judged for their work. But the interpretations of our performance by other people should never be our motivating force. When we work, we are working for God, and He takes note of what we do for Him.

Demon spirits will regularly use religious people to accuse authentic church members of being the problem in society or the Church. They want true Christians to think they are unwell, when in fact, they are the ones who are sick and need to be healed of their impure religious traditions. Religious demons accuse the child of God of being problematic and a disruption, yet we know we are the agents of change, bringing hope and healing to all who want to be healed, if we have properly learned and followed the teachings of God. We know they themselves could be set free if only they admitted their error and repented for their wrongdoing.

Demons hated Elijah and his work, and they wanted to silence the voice of God from revealing their wicked deeds and wicked society. Today, the same demons hate us and accuse us of causing chaos and problems for the church, or the mainstream society, when in fact they are the ones who have unholy and unjust rulings and practices in place for the people. First Kings 18:17-18 explains, *"When he saw Elijah, he said to him, "Is that you, you troubler of Israel?" "I have not made trouble for Israel," Elijah replied. "But you and your father's family have. You have abandoned the Lord's commands and have followed the Baals."* (NIV)

Today there are demonic demonstrations and philosophies being bred and taught by those who are deceived by Satan. These devils want to stop the work of God and weaken the body of Christ. Yet, those of us who are free and willing to contribute to the kingdom of God can reveal them. When we commit to God and His Word, we will find ourselves in the right place at the right time, demonstrating to the world the pure and holy script of God to those who are willing to watch, learn, and imitate.

We don't perform God's work alone. In one moment of exhaustion, Elijah thought he was alone in his ministry, but he wasn't. God had people who needed him to be strong as their leader. Other believers need us. Let us rise up to lead with passion and conviction teaching the pure word of the Lord, so we can train children sound in their faith and strong and healthy in their minds, bodies, and spirits. Having a moment of exhaustion or ignorance as a authentic Christian leader isn't God's best for our lives, but the true leader will receive God's instruction and edification in those moments and will once again rise to continue the work.

First Kings 19:14-18 says, *"He said, I have been very jealous for the Lord God of hosts, because the Israelites have forsaken Your covenant, thrown down Your altars, and slain Your prophets with the sword. And I, I only, am left, and they seek my life, to destroy it. And the Lord said to him, Go, return on your way to the Wilderness of Damascus; and when you arrive, anoint Hazael to be king over Syria. And anoint Jehu son of Nimshi to be king over Israel, and anoint Elisha son of Shaphat of Abel-meholah to be prophet in your place. And him who escapes from the sword of Hazael Jehu shall slay, and him who escapes the sword of Jehu Elisha shall slay. Yet I will leave Myself 7,000 in Israel, all the knees that have not bowed to Baal and every mouth that has not kissed him."* (AMPC)

7

Feminism's Ungodly Roots

Some women proudly assert themselves as feminists. A feminist is said to advocate on behalf of women and their rights. Feminists believe their efforts to define and establish political, personal, economic, and social equality of the sexes will improve the lives of women in the present age, as well as in the future.

However, many women find themselves joining themselves to a movement with hidden facets and impressions. Feminism on the surface appears to be beneficial and harmless, but as we look deeper into its origins, we can see the corruption and moral filth associated with the feminist movement.

Reptiles are animals notorious for hiding and concealing their identities. Almost all reptile species, from the alligator to chameleons, find ease in concealing themselves until they are ready to attack. Most reptiles use camouflage to blend in with their surroundings so they can avoid detection by their predators or by their prey. Camouflage is a way to gain power and social standing, it is a way to gain advantage.

In the same way, the devil and his demons commonly hide their identity from their prey: the un-discerning humans who are their predators. Although some demons aggressively present themselves, not all do. Many demons camouflage themselves so people will comply with them and join them, oftentimes without knowing it. Within the feminist movement, we see both covert and the unmistakable demons at work. Some philosophies of feminists are bold and blatantly evil and destructive, while others are more cunning.

Feminism is often broken into time periods called *waves*. Generally, the eras categorizing the movement are the first wave, second wave, third wave, and fourth wave. Most scholars believe the first wave of feminism began in the 1800s, led by Lucretia Mott and Elizabeth Cady Stanton. Mott and Stanton advocated that all men and women were created equal, so women had the right to education, property, and organizational leadership.

These goals were assumed to be addressed through the woman's right to vote. Thus, voting became one initial primary goal of the first wave. These goals are honorable and understandable, as God wants His daughters to have the right to land ownership, to education, and to leadership positions. He also wants women to have a voice within politics to select the proper American leadership.

However, beneath these seemingly innocent agendas, there was another spirit warring for the mind, heart, and soul of the woman. And deeper analysis of the current feminist movement shows us who is behind feminism and who feminists really are.

Consider, for instance, the impact of women's suffrage on the dynamics of the husband-wife relationship. Before the suffrage movement, couples typically made electoral decisions together, presenting a united front. However, the introduction of women's right to vote transformed this paradigm, allowing both women and men within the same household to develop individual identities and aspirations; a dangerous thing for marriage and family.

Amos 3:3 teaches, *"Do two walk together unless they have agreed to do so?"*

Christians are called to walk in harmony with Christ, meant to be yoked together with Him, ultimately progressing in the same direction while heeding His guidance. Similarly, the union between a woman and a man should adhere to this principle. In marriage, both partners are yoked together; if they do not walk in unison toward a common goal, they are heading towards disaster. Although subtle, this path to destruction invariably undermines the truth. Little by little and step by step the *two* meant to be *one* separate.

Feminists are not God-fearing women. They are willing to achieve power and status by any means possible. Feminists are willing to lie, steal, and cheat to gain an advantage. They are willing to override God's standards of truth. They don't play by the rules, and these characteristics are not those of a Christian woman.

In Proverbs 31:16-17, a godly woman works hard, learns and gains strength, buys property, and leads others in her sphere of influence. Godly women have power and influence, but they don't achieve it through corruption and affiliation with evil.

"She considers a field before she buys or accepts it [expanding her business prudently]; With her profits she plants fruitful vines in her vineyard. She equips herself with strength [spiritual, mental, and physical fitness for her God-given task] And makes her arms strong." (AMPC)

God wants women to be wise, through education and learning, and He wants us to assert ourselves in powerful and influential positions. Operating in faith and honor toward God blesses our households and communities. We are a blessing to our children, our husbands, and our community. The Christian woman's aspirations are to impact her home and society through godliness and holiness before the Lord our God, because when we partner with God and His Word, we can generate positive change and impact.

"She tastes and sees that her gain from work [with and for God] is good; her lamp goes not out, but it burns on continually through the night [of trouble, privation, or sorrow, warning away fear, doubt, and distrust]. She lays her hands to the spindle, and her hands hold the distaff. She opens her hand to the poor, yes, she reaches out her filled hands to the needy [whether in body, mind, or spirit]. She fears not the snow for her family, for all her household are doubly clothed in scarlet. She makes for herself coverlets, cushions, and rugs of tapestry.

Her clothing is of linen, pure and fine, and of purple [such as that of which the clothing of the priests and the hallowed cloths of the temple were made]. Her husband is known in the [city's] gates, when he sits among the elders of the land. She makes fine linen garments and leads others to buy them; she delivers to the merchants girdles [or sashes that free one up for service]. Strength and dignity are her clothing and her position is strong and secure; she rejoices over the future [the latter day or time to come, knowing that she and her family are in readiness for it]" (Proverbs 31:18-25, Amplified)!

Because of Christian women's commitment to and work for God, they will be blessed and praised. Godly women operate in unison with God, who never fails. As we submit to His leadership, His wisdom, and His direction, we are guaranteed to be successful in all we do. Submission to God through fear and admiration is the key that unlocks prosperity and blessing.

Her children rise up and call her blessed (happy, fortunate, and to be envied); and her husband boasts of and praises her, [saying], Many daughters have done virtuously, nobly, and well [with the strength of character that is steadfast in goodness], but you excel them all. Charm and grace are deceptive, and beauty is vain [because it is not lasting], but a woman who reverently and worshipfully fears the Lord, she shall be praised! Give her of the fruit of her hands, and let her own works praise her in the gates [of the city]! (Proverbs 31:28-31) (AMPC)

Doing business with a woman of like minded faith brings no contention. But godly women will find strife, abuse, mismanagement, and mistreatment among those who are not godly themselves, and in these scenarios, women need the Holy Spirit's divine insight and protection.

Women in Scripture were commended for usurping male leadership if their leader was making foolish, ungodly decisions. Abigail was one of the women the Lord approved for going against the ruling of her husband. Abigail properly discerned David as a servant of the Lord, so she acted humbly in faith out of fear and reverence to God, even when this decision was one of disobedience to her husband Nabal.

First Samuel 25:17 explains, "*So know this and consider what you will do, for evil is determined against our master and all his house. For he is such a wicked man that one cannot speak to him. Then Abigail made haste and took 200 loaves, two skins of wine, five sheep already dressed, five measures of parched grain, 100 clusters of raisins, and 200 cakes of figs, and laid them on donkeys. And she said to her servants, Go on before me; behold, I come after you. But she did not tell her husband Nabal.*" (AMPC)

Abigail noted she could not speak to her husband. This tells us he was unwilling to include her into his decisions. He locked her out of the decision making process and he negated her as an important voice within the house. This behavior from a husband was inappropriate, because God instructs men to be considerate of their wives. He commands all Christians to lead in authority considering others more valuable than themselves. *"Do nothing out of selfish ambition or vain conceit. Rather, in humility value others above yourself"* (Philippians 2:3, NIV).

A fool refuses to hear the words of the Lord and heed them with reverence and admiration. God's word and truth isn't for us to like or dislike. It is the final authority whether we approve of it or not. Yet foolish people believe they are superior to God, His Word, and His people. They refuse to submit and humble themselves before the very God who gives them their life, because out of pride they think they know better, and this belief contributes to poor decision making.

Let not my lord, I pray you, regard this foolish and wicked fellow Nabal, for as his name is, so is he—Nabal [foolish, wicked] is his name, and folly is with him. But I, your handmaid, did not see my lord's young men whom you sent. So now, my lord, as the Lord lives and as your soul lives, seeing that the Lord has prevented you from bloodguiltiness and from avenging yourself with your own hand, now let your enemies and those who seek to do evil to my lord be as Nabal (First Samuel 25:25-26) (AMPC)

Men who fail to honor and treat their wife in accordance with the scriptures are also following their own way rebelling against God. Husbands must treat their wives well to receive God's favor, blessing, and help. Without properly caring for your wife you will never prosper any further in God. God assures us that man's prayers will be hindered.

Some foolish leaders within and churches have lulled inexperienced Christians to sleep preaching a doctrine of devils training people to remain yoked and joined to lifestyles of sin, in unison with a confession of faith and belief in Jesus Christ. By not fearing and respecting the raw truths of the word of God, these leaders teach a false doctrine because they believe they are above the standards of God, and are superior to submission and authority.

To remain hidden, these demons pretend to not be there, promising life alongside rebellion. These demon spirits hide in the Church; the very place most un-discerning people won't even see them. Like a snake hiding on a tree branch or a crocodile slightly below the surface of the water, these beasts wait and watch to devour all who don't see them and rebuke them. *Be alert and of sober mind. Your enemy the devil prowls around like a roaring lion looking for someone to devour.* (First Peter 5:8, NIV).

Using some religious behavior in combination with evil, Satan traps the ignorant. The lie appears good. It appeals to our human reasoning and ears, but it is a lie nonetheless. Second Corinthians 11:12-15 explains, *"And I will keep on doing what I am doing in order to cut the ground from under those who want an opportunity to be considered equal with us in the things they boast about. For such people are false apostles, deceitful workers, masquerading as apostles of Christ. And no wonder, for Satan himself masquerades as an angel of light. It is not surprising, then, if his servants also masquerade as servants of righteousness. Their end will be what their actions deserve."* (NIV)

According to this scripture believers and unbelievers are not equal; as God esteems the believer to be on a higher level than those who are not believers. Abigail was operating in faith and was a believer. Her husband Nabal was not, so although he felt as if he was superior to her and he believed he was in a leadership position over her, in reality he was not. That is why the Lord rewarded her for her behavior, because she was not acting out of proper authority- she was operating within it.

While certainly many of the ideals of the feminist movement incorporate concepts of justice and goodness, they are humanistic at best and demonic at worst. Feminism is polluted, contaminated and tainted at its core. It is a philosophy, full of half-truths, demonic lies, promising women that rebellion and anarchy is better than submission and contentment. Feminism is not about freedom, justice, and respect. It is about no authority, government, or law. It is a movement of lawlessness and hatred toward God.

Feminism promises freedom and fullness of life alongside rebellion and it leads to destruction. This movement exalts itself against the word of God. It positions itself with the enemy yet conceals itself as a righteous movement intended on improving the lives of those who follow it.

Second Corinthians 11:16-21 explains, "*I say again, let no one think me a fool. If otherwise, at least receive me as a fool, that I also may boast a little. What I speak, I speak not according to the Lord, but as it were, foolishly, in this confidence of boasting. Seeing that many boast according to the flesh, I also will boast. For you put up with fools gladly, since you yourselves are wise! For you put up with it if one brings you into bondage, if one devours you, if one takes from you, if one exalts himself, if one strikes you on the face. To our shame I say that we were too weak for that! But in whatever anyone is bold—I speak foolishly—I am bold also.*" (NIV)

James 2:19 also tells us, "*You believe that there is one God. You do well. Even the demons believe—and tremble!*" (NIV) A belief and even a confession in the reality of God does not constitute salvation. A belief or a confession of faith, without works —and corresponding behavior and actions — is the same as death and rebellion. To receive our salvation and walk out our faith, we must believe, confess, and behave in accordance with our confession of faith. "*So too, faith, if it does not have works [to back it up], is by itself dead [inoperative and ineffective]*" (James 2:17, Amplified).

What we do, and the fruit we manifest from our lives is the evidence of our salvation and transformation through Christ Jesus. If we have been born again and properly trained in the word of God we will bear the image of our Father. We will begin to manifest the characteristics of heaven, not hell.

In Matthew 7:15-20 Jesus says, "*Watch out for false prophets. They come to you in sheep's clothing, but inwardly they are ferocious wolves. By their fruit you will recognize them. Do people pick grapes from thornbushes, or figs from thistles? Likewise, every good tree bears good fruit, but a bad tree bears bad fruit. A good tree cannot bear bad fruit, and a bad tree cannot bear good fruit. Every tree that does not bear good fruit is cut down and thrown into the fire. Thus, by their fruit you will recognize them.*" (NIV)

To be false, a person must assert themselves to be true. Wolves are not unsaved worldly people. Wolves are people who assert themselves to be members of Christ's body. They are those who lie to deceive and destroy the sheep within God's flock. Jesus says in Matthew 7:21-23, "*Not everyone who says to Me, Lord, Lord, will enter the kingdom of heaven, but he who does the will of My Father Who is in heaven. Many will say to Me on that day, Lord, Lord, have we not prophesied in Your name and driven out demons in Your name and done many mighty works in Your name? And then I will say to them openly (publicly), I never knew you; depart from Me, you who act wickedly [disregarding My commands].*" (AMPC)

Obedience to God and His Word are introductory aspects of the Christian life. When there is rebellion and disregard to God and His commands, there is witchcraft and sorcery lurking right below the surface. We cannot be sinners and rebellious and be saved and sanctified creatures in Christ. Romans 6:6 says, "*We know that our old self [our human nature without the Holy Spirit] was nailed to the cross with Him, in* order that our body of sin might be done away with, so that we would no longer be slaves to sin." (AMPC)

As we become new creatures, fully yoked with Jesus Christ, we are one with Him and correspondingly, one with the Father in heaven. We are on the same mission, and we are no longer on the same mission as sinners and Satan. In agriculture, a yoke joins two creatures/workers of the field together. The yoke keeps the two workers going in the same direction, in one mind and accord. As the two work together, the fields are cultivated to produce an abundant crop.

Professing to be a Christian, yet denying the Lord's headship, is to be unequally yoked, something we are warned of in Scripture. God-fearing women will willingly step out of poor leadership instructions in reverence to God and His Word, because we must honor our Lord above all men on the earth. Being yoked with Christ sometimes requires us to break company with people who are not yoked with Him too!

Plans made by society, the devil, or mankind in opposition to God's plan must be resisted. Authority asserting itself against God and His authority must be severed and usurped for us to remain in unison and obedience to God. Some people, organizations, and systems force us to choose God over them because they refuse to cooperate with Him and His mission.

A tiny bit of poison in your drinking water can still kill you. The Holy Spirit will warn us and inform us when we are in the company of our enemy. God wants us to stay on track. He wants us to never be led astray or deceived by our enemy. But we must be willing and obedient to cut our associations with ungodly people and doctrines.

Joshua 23:9-13 explains,

"The Lord has driven out before you great and powerful nations; to this day no one has been able to withstand you. One of you routs a thousand, because the Lord your God fights for you, just as he promised. " So be very careful to love the Lord your God.

"But if you turn away and ally yourselves with the survivors of these nations that remain among you and if you intermarry with them and associate with them, then you may be sure that the Lord your God will no longer drive out these nations before you. Instead, they will become snares and traps for you, whips on your backs and thorns in your eyes, until you perish from this good land, which the Lord your God has given you." (NIV)

I want the best for women, and I refuse to break bread and make an alliance with anyone or any group that doesn't share in the interests of Christ's kingdom I am a part of. I know God's kingdom has women's best interest in mind. God's statues and regulations are the superior standard and outcome for all women. Therefore, standing with a political group, movement, person, or self-serving interest like feminism means standing with the enemy and standing against the hand of God, and this would be personally and publicly destructive.

Abigail could have remained in her husband's household, silent and unwilling to address and confront his wicked heart. But if she had, she would have been slaughtered with the rest of the house. All of the spirits and the people around her would have witnessed her choice and her consequence.

The alliances we make matter. Our covenant with God is a promise and a blood oath to operate, behave, and contribute to the fight with the enemy through our alliance with God. God doesn't take our word lightly. We need to ensure we aren't liars, believing we can usurp God or fool Him when He is the one who made our heart and gives us breath.

As Joshua told Israel, *"If you transgress the covenant of the Lord your God, which He commanded you, and go and serve other gods and bow down to them, then the anger of the Lord will burn against you, and you will quickly perish from this good land He has given you"* (Joshua 23:16, NIV).

Beneath the surface of feminism lies demon spirits. They hide from the ignorant and the rebellious mind so they can control a life through an unholy alliance. Today, in the fourth wave, many of these demons are arrogantly showing themselves. Not all devils hide, especially when they are confronted and feel threatened. In America today, many Christians are fighting back against these unclean spirits, and as a result, they are screaming back, trying to intimate anyone who is unsure of their identity in Christ.

Demons seek to compel individuals to choose a side, presenting humanity with the option to align either with God or with them in adherence to evil. When individuals fail to reject and denounce evil, they inadvertently become complicit, even if they claim innocence. As stated in James 4:17, *"Therefore, to him who knows to do good and does not do it, to him it is sin."* (NIV)

Whose voice do we hear so abrasively today on the street? It isn't the voice of the Lord. It is the voice of feminism. The right to kill babies, the desire to be promiscuous whores, lesbianism, and other willful transgressions of God's plan for womanhood. A outright hatred and rebellion of husbands and men at large rumble through the streets in the name of feminism. Only a fool would be willing to side with this movement and turn a blind eye to truth and justice. As only a devious, God-hating demon filled, man, or woman would demonstrate this form of vile and disgusting fruit.

"Here is my servant whom I have chosen, the one I love, in whom I delight; I will put my Spirit on him, and he will proclaim justice to the nations. He will not quarrel or cry out; no one will hear his voice in the streets" (Matthew 12:18-19, NIV).

8

Domineering & Destructive
Doctrines of Devils

Jesus is the Lord of the Sabbath.
Jesus Christ: The Son of Man and the Lord of Law and Justice.
"At that time Jesus went through the grainfields on the Sabbath. His disciples were hungry and began to pick some heads of grain and eat them. When the Pharisees saw this, they said to him, "Look! Your disciples are doing what is unlawful on the Sabbath." He answered, "Haven't you read what David did when he and his companions were hungry? He entered the house of God, and he is and his companions ate the consecrated bread-which was not lawful for them to do, but only for the priests. Or haven't you read in the Law that the priests on Sabbath duty in the temple desecrate the Sabbath and yet are innocent? I tell you that something greater than the temple is here. If you had known what these words mean, 'I desire mercy, not sacrifice,' you would have not condemned the innocent. For the Son of Man is the Lord of the Sabbath."

Going on from that place, he went into their synagogue, and a man with a shriveled hand was there. Looking for a reason to bring charges against Jesus, they asked him, "Is it lawful to heal on the Sabbath?" He said to them, "If any of you has a sheep and it falls into a pit on the Sabbath, will you not take hold of it and lift it out? How much more valuable is a person than a sheep! Therefore it is lawful to heal on the Sabbath." Then he said to the man, "Stretch out your hand." So he stretched it out and it was completely restored, just as sound as the other. But the Pharisees went out and plotted how they might kill Jesus" (Matthew 12:1-14 NIV).

The religious demons' first response in attempting to stop and control Jesus' was through twisting the law. Satan and demon spirits frequently use Scripture and biblical language to intimidate or manipulate those fighting against them. These spirits take believers to the courts of law to try to find fault in them; as Jesus was taken to court before He was sentenced to death.

Religious leaders deceived and following religious spirits, manifest the demonic through an incorrect interpretation of God's laws. Throughout all of history, the lack of proper interpretation of the law has caused religious men and women to harm innocent people. Christians have been persecuted or killed and have been drug into courts of law to be accused of wrongdoing, and evil spirits are behind these operations every single time.

Saint Stephen, as many other disciples, was taken into a court room before he was killed. Acts 7 tells us, "Then the high priest asked Stephen, 'Are these charges true?'" (AMPC)

Throughout Christian history, men and women have been persecuted and killed through the twisting of religious law. It shouldn't come as a surprise to us today that those submitting to devils will at times use the Word of God as a weapon to pervert true justice and truth, because this has always been a part of Satan's tactic to destroy Christians. The Word of God is a weapon, and evil spirits want to use it as a weapon for evil, not good.

Satan and his army regularly disguise themselves as spirits of truth. As in days past, religious leaders spread false doctrine and hate in the present age, and they believe they are standing with God, but they are standing against Him. Revelation 16:14 says, "For really they are the spirits of demons that perform signs (wonders, miracles). And they go forth to the rulers and leaders all over the world, to gather them together for war on the great day of God the Almighty." (AMPC)

Jesus taught on the value of life and humanity. He healed and de-livered people from affliction and bondage. Jesus' objective was deliverance from evil for anyone who was willing to believe He was able to save them even from death.

Religious leaders such as the Pharisees always despised God's assertion that all people, under all circumstances and through faith, can be delivered from their bondage and afflictions through Christ. Still today, many religious people feel it is their duty to keep people from their salvation, healing, or help because they deem them unworthy and unfit for salvation and assistance from God.

In Matthew 12:4, the verse that initiated our discussion in this chapter, Jesus references David and his men consuming the conse-crated bread, which was typically reserved for priests. In ancient Is-rael, the showbread, also known as the Bread of the Presence, held a significant place of honor. However, when David and his men found themselves in a state of war and in dire need of sustenance, God per-mitted them to partake of the bread, recognizing their need for sur-vival. Had they not consumed the showbread, they might have faced defeat in battle.

This scripture illustrates not only the importance of triumphing in spiritual battles but also reveals that God may allow certain individ-uals to access divine provisions, even when they do not meet conven-tional qualifications in the physical realm. God deemed David worthy of the showbread, just as He recognized Abigail as a leader within her household, as discussed in the previous chapter. This understand-ing emphasizes that God alone determines who is granted authority and position. He possesses the ability to discern our spiritual identity, which is distinct from our natural identity.

Jesus addressed religious demons and the misinterpretation of Scriptures directly. He taught religious leaders' proper interpretation of Scripture so they could see their twisted interpretation was unjust. Religious law improperly applied is harmful and enslaving to mankind. It keeps certain groups from attaining the promises God has for all who will believe. Religious people deceived by religious demons would rather a person die than live. They would rather leave a man suffering and in need of healing than to see the man healed and set free on the Sabbath. And they would rather an entire army pursuing God's plan and purposes lose the war than to grant access to one they inaccurately perceive as less than themselves.

A lack of compassion for others and a resistant spirit that denies it's support in all people benefiting from their relationship with God indicates that one's heart is not in tune with God's Spirit. Authentic believers who have been saved and sanctified know we, too, were once unworthy. We admit we needed Jesus to save us, and it was not due to our own works that we were saved. This understanding of salvation through grace, not works, is the key that helps us to minister to the lost without hatred and unfair judgment. It allows us to preach, teach, and love others regardless of who we think that they are.

God is the healer, the deliverer and the Savior. He is the God of love and salvation to all mankind. Jesus died on the cross for the sins of the world, and He is allowing more people to come to experience salvation through His patient and kind nature. Our job as the Church is to present the truth to all people and to hope they come to the knowledge of the truth. We are not gatekeepers of the kingdom; Jesus alone is the one who opens or shuts the doors.

The religious spirit operates in some churches - our modern synagogues. These synagogues of Satan operate under demon spirits and hate the deliverance work of The Church of Jesus Christ. Religious demons and religious people mock teachings on deliverance, healing, and miracles as they have always done. They still believe they are in right standing with God because of their works and their public proclamation. Yet in their hearts they are opposed to the demonstration of the Holy Spirit and the works of God.

The authentic Church of Jesus Christ casts out demons, heals the sick, and delivers people from all manners of sickness and disease and oppression. These objectives were given by Jesus, and His Church will manifest them, regardless of those who don't like it, because Jesus Christ is the head of the Church and He makes the standard of right and wrong. We don't determine the mission of the Church. Jesus is in charge, and we can either work with Him or against Him.

"And He said to them, "Go into all the world and preach the gospel to all creation. He who has believed [in Me] and has been baptized will be saved [from the penalty of God's wrath and judgment]; but he who has not believed will be condemned. These signs will accompany those who have believed: in My name they will cast out demons, they will speak in new tongues; they will pick up serpents, and if they drink anything deadly, it will not hurt them; they will lay hands on the sick, and they will get well. So then, when the Lord Jesus had spoken to them, He was taken up into heaven and sat down at the right hand of God" (Mark 16:15-19, Amplified).

To cast out means to forcibly remove the enemy. Casting out involves throwing out anything that is endangering the boat to become sunken or shipwrecked. When we cast out devils and all forms of evil, we are protecting the people/the vessels. This is the mission of Jesus.

Religious demons need to be dealt with and addressed, not ignored and permitted to rule and reign in churches. Christians need to understand what a religious demon is and they need to learn how to deal with them. If possible, these spirits will tempt and lure believers into their way of thinking and behaving. They will lead the believer astray and cause them to bring shame and harm to those in God's house.

Religious demons raise their head against those who operate in the anointing of God, trying first to slander and accuse, then to full out murder the anointed saint. Accusations and insinuations of wrongdoing, through misunderstanding the mind of God, leads to persecution and, when possible, full out martyrdom. In the United States, it is illegal to kill, so the religious people living in this country result to slander and violence using their tongues for evil.

The tongue is a powerful weapon, and at times, individuals wield their words as weapons, even against those God considers His family within their religious communities. Jesus told us if we hate in our heart, we are guilty of murder. The brothers and sisters pretending to be a part of the Church, who hate their brothers and sisters for operating in the anointing, are guilty of murdering their brothers/sisters. This is the spirit of Cain. It is the spirit of the Pharisee.

In our contemporary society, the individuals who resemble the Pharisees of old, use their platforms within the Church to demean, belittle, and degrade others while asserting to be performing God's work. Slander, a sin frequently overlooked in contemporary society, constitutes a serious offense against both the Lord and fellow members of His community. It is defined as a false spoken statement that damages an individual's reputation or standing within the community.

When Christians use their tongues to damage another Christian's ministry, name, or reputation without reason they are guilty of slander. With the rise of social media we are seeing many people using their platforms for evil. While asserting themselves as Christians these people gossip about, lie about, and belittle other Christians. Their entire "ministry" is often a ministry of "exposing" wolves in the Church-- when what they are really doing is working against the Church as an agent of Satan.

Religious demons often employ slander as a means to create division within the Church. If Satan can incite Christians to turn against one another, he effectively undermines the unity of those who should be collaborating in their shared faith to combat him.

We should never tolerate people who constantly gossip and cause divisions. In addition, these types of people should never be trusted and followed when given leadership roles. Individuals within the Church who create problems and stir up drama need to be addressed and many times removed from the Church. This action is done to protect the authentic sheep from the damage and the ravenous nature of the wolf in sheep's clothing. Ministers should be able to recognize a person carrying a religious demon because God has anointed us to.

First Peter 2:1 says, *"So put away all malice and all deceit and hypocrisy and envy and all slander."* (ESV) Exodus 20:16 teaches, *"You shall not bear false witness against your neighbor."* (ESV) And James 4:11-12 explains, *"Do not speak evil against one another, brothers. The one who speaks against a brother or judges his brother, speaks evil against the law and judges the law. But if you judge the law, you are not a doer of the law but a judge. There is only one lawgiver and judge, he who is able to save and to destroy. But who are you to judge your neighbor?"* (ESV)

Demons have no place within the house of God. Just as we must cultivate a life devoid of evil, our places of worship should also reflect this commitment. We cannot permit Satan to feel at ease among us. The fire of God serves to dispel malevolent spirits, casting out all forms of evil. When we remain spiritually fervent, the majority of demonic forces will flee in fear, for we embody the Spirit of God. And those spirits who remain and are generally the religious spirits can be forced to depart when they are confronted and commanded to go! This aspect of ministry represents a fundamental role of the Church; one we must never forget about.

Ezra 10:1-8 teaches, *"Now while Ezra prayed and made confession, weeping and casting himself down before the house of God, there gathered to him out of Israel a very great assembly of men, women, and children; for the people wept bitterly. And Shecaniah [II] son of Jehiel [one of the congregation], of the sons of Elam, said to Ezra: We have broken faith and dealt treacherously against our God and have married foreign women of the peoples of the land; yet now there is still hope for Israel in spite of this thing. Therefore let us make a covenant with our God to put away all the foreign wives and their children, according to the counsel of my lord and of those who tremble at the command of our God; and let it be done according to the Law. Arise, for it is your duty, and we are with you. Be strong and brave and do it.*

Then Ezra arose and made the chiefs of the priests, the Levites, and all Israel swear that they would do as had been said. So they took the oath. Then Ezra came from before the house of God and went into the lodging place of Jehohanan son of Eliashib [for the night]. There he ate no bread and drank no water, for he mourned over the returned exiles' faithlessness [and violation of God's law]. And proclamation was made throughout Judah and Jerusalem to

all the returned exiles, that they should assemble in Jerusalem, And that who-
ever did not come within three days, by order of the officials and the elders,
all his property should be forfeited and he himself banned from the assembly
of the exiles." (AMPC)

As a spiritual leader, Ezra confronted the men under his leadership and his stance on sin contributed to the men repenting for their sin. In the same way, all leaders in the Church are under oath to teach the people the truth of God's Word. We are in a covenant, command- ing us to preach the whole counsel of God's Word. If the people are not taught and warned of their sin and their misconduct against God, their blood is on the hands of those who omitted the truth, refusing to perform their God-ordained ministry.

Ezra influenced the people positively. He mourned for the sin within the people, and he warned them of their sins against God. As the people saw Ezra's genuine mourning, they were confronted with their need to be cleansed. They realized they needed to repent and change their behavior to be holy before the Lord. The choice is clear: Leaders can lead the people into further sin and separation from God, or they can stand up before the people and proclaim righteousness and truth.

Ministers can set a standard that pleases the Father and changes nations through their reverent passion and commitment to truth. Pe- ter gives this reminder: *"because it is written, "You shall be Holy (set apart), For I am Holy." If you address as Father, the One who impartially judges according to each one's work, conduct yourselves in [reverent] fear [of Him] and with profound respect for Him throughout the time of your stay on earth"* (First Peter 1:16-17, Amplified).

Demon spirits within religious atmospheres want to corrupt the leadership first so they can spread poison to the people. That's why we must never become tolerant casual regarding sin because if leaders become passive, they will inherently pass these attitudes on to the people. Leaders must never fall asleep and make little mention of the supernatural aspects of true religion and devotion to God. To do so would be to give the devil an opportunity to hurt God's people.

Jesus came to fulfill the law. His life, death, and resurrection help us to live above the standard of holiness, not beneath it. Christians live by a higher moral code with higher standards. Our standards are even higher than those who attest themselves to be upright and religious.

"For I say to you that unless your righteousness (uprightness, moral essence) is more than that of the scribes and Pharisees, you will never enter the kingdom of heaven. "You have heard that it was said to the men of old, 'You shall not murder' and 'whoever murders shall be guilty before the court. But I say to you that everyone who continues to be angry with his brother or harbors malice (enmity of heart) against him shall be liable to and unable to escape the punishment imposed by the court; and whoever speaks contemptuously and insultingly to his brother shall be liable to and unable to escape the punishment imposed by the Sanhedrin, and whoever says, You cursed fool! [You empty-headed idiot!] shall be liable to and unable to escape the hell (Gehenna) of fire. " (Matthew 5:20-22, Amplified).

Demons in the Church are left-handed spirits. They are warrior demons accustomed to deceiving and destroying people who are unprepared for them to attack in an atmosphere such as the Church. Not everyone within the churches are to be trusted, because not everyone who claims to be a son of Abraham- a Christian truly is one. Yet young Christians not accustomed to fighting with religious demons may be taken off guard and defeated, through the unsuspected attack.

Christians without experience and without proper guidance can believe and be led astray by leaders who mishandle God's Word. Therefore it is essential for us as the Church to preach, teach, and explain the Bible clearly and boldly. We must never hold back the fire of God and the sword of the Spirit in our ministries, because we can help those the enemy wants to lure away from God when we move in power and authority with Jesus.

Jesus sits on the right side of the Father. To experience salvation and to operate within God's kingdom we must start on the right side of God, not the left. The right side of God is associated with Jesus, as well as the law, the truth, and justice. When we fail to understand the significance of holiness and the submission to the laws of God, we cannot progress spiritually into deeper aspects of the faith. If we are going to be saved and productive citizens of God's kingdom, we must start on the right side with Jesus and repentance of our violations of the law.

On the left side, there is grace, forgiveness of sin, and mercy. However, this is only accessed through a full understanding and submission to the law and the holy standards of God. When we come to Jesus, we must acknowledge, confess and confront the reality of our sinful nature. We must be humble and willing to see ourselves as imperfect and in need of salvation because of our transgressions. We will experience the grace of God, once we have first experienced the need for that grace.

A humble heart, in contrast to a proud one, acknowledges our need for a sacrifice before God. Abel exemplified this humility by willingly offering a sacrifice for his sins, demonstrating his acknowledgment of the necessity for God's forgiveness and grace. This posture of the heart facilitated a close relationship with the Lord, unlike his brother Cain, who failed to adopt the same humility.

Religious demons trick people to believe they can get to God without an understanding of the law and without the proper sacrifice for their sins. Cain believed God should accept him even though he refused to obey God's commands. He sought to approach God through pride in his own perceived righteousness. Religious people deceived by Satan deem themselves worthy although they are not.

A left-handed religious spirit distorts religion by teaching an inaccurate grace message, such as continuing to sin without seeking forgiveness. These doctrines promise people salvation without changing lifestyles and behaviors. Left-handed spirits tell their victims they are safe and forgiven, though they haven't repented or stopped sinning. And since these demonically encoded messages are often spoken by "ministers" of the gospel, many hearers will be deceived and go to hell for believing these lies.

Left-handed spirits twist the law in the name of religion. Through improper analysis and understanding of Scripture, many will believe they are on the side of justice, as they did when they killed Jesus, but indeed they are on the side of the guilty. Religious people refuse to admit they have contributed to evil against God. Both now and in the past, they have been taken out by left-handed spirits and don't see the attack because it is disguised as the truth of God.

The twisting of the law and the misunderstanding of grace and holiness lead men and women to never repent of their sins. Religious people and those never properly taught to fear the Lord because of the failure of leaders in the Church to confront sin will cause people to falsely believe they don't need to change anything or repent, because they are safe in their stance with the Lord when indeed they are not.

The religious spirits' entire objective with these two doctrines is to keep people from a saving relationship with God. People who are tricked will have failed to properly perceive and repent of wrongdoing, and this lack of repentance is what will keep them from salvation.

We can see how Jesus felt about repentance in this familiar story:

"But Jesus went to the Mount of Olives. At dawn he appeared again in the temple courts, where all the people gathered around him, and he sat down to teach them. The teachers of the law and the Pharisees brought in a woman caught in adultery. They made her stand before the group and said to Jesus, "Teacher, this woman was caught in the act of adultery. In the Law Moses commanded us to stone such women. Now what do you say?" They were using this question as a trap, in order to have a basis for accusing him.

But Jesus bent down and started to write on the ground with his finger. When they kept on questioning him, he straightened up and said to them, "Let any one of you who is without sin be the first to throw a stone at her." Again he stooped down and wrote on the ground. At this, those who heard began to go away one at a time, the older ones first, until only Jesus was left, with the woman still standing there. Jesus straightened up and asked her, "Woman, where are they? Has no one condemned you?" "No one, sir," she said. "Then neither do I condemn you," Jesus declared. "Go now and leave your life of sin" (John 8:1-11 NIV).

God wants us to live holy. Jesus told the accused woman to stop sinning. Refusing to continue to live within a lifestyle of sin is a part of our salvation and rebirth. Following the law and trying to live blamelessly without Jesus isn't enough. We can't earn our way to heaven by our good works. We must realize we were not able to meet the standards of God without Jesus Christ. We must realize that apart from Christ, we can't be justified before God.

Relying fully on Jesus Christ as Savior is the only way to heaven. He is the way the truth and the life, the key that unlocks the door. Once we have His help and His Spirit, we are free indeed and no longer in bondage to a corrupted lifestyle. We can choose to sin no more, because His Spirit and our new nature permits us with special access to freedom and God's grace!

For the human brain to work properly, we need the left and the right hemispheres. The left side is responsible for logic, language, processing, and analytical thinking. The right side is responsible for our creative and subjective thinking. When people experience a brain injury, they are usually limited in one of the two sides of the brain, and their behavior is skewed. Likewise, a person without a full understanding of law and grace is skewed. They are not fully seeing and interpreting the Scriptures in the way they were written.

God designed our brains to be renewed and sanctified by the Word. He created us to be balanced on the right and the left so we can truly understand Him and His plan. On one hand, God is the God of law and order. He is the God who requires an adherence to the law. On the other hand, He is forgiving and merciful. He is a Savior and a helper to us if we accidentally violate His standards, because He is our Creator, the God of grace.

The human left hand is controlled by the right hemisphere of the brain, and the right is controlled by the left hemisphere. When we encounter left-handed demon spirits, we fight spirits whose domain relates to emotion and intuition. We are fighting spirits who want us to believe and trust in ourselves and our own understanding or beliefs.

That is precisely why these demons hate the work of the Holy Spirit. He unveils the supernatural to God's people, intervening to dismantle the extraordinary challenges in our lives. The Holy Spirit eradicates our dependence on human understanding and logic, guiding us to place our trust in God and His divine purposes and plans rather than our own.

God is not disabled. He has two hands. If we want to know God, we must seek to understand every part of who He is. A failure to know God in His entirety results in an unbalanced and unhealthy view of Him. As laborers in the field of God, we need to be on the lookout for the religious demon spirits of law and the demon spirits of false grace. Both are used against the Church to destroy it from within, so we must cast them out before they hurt a single sheep. If these spirits are left unchecked, they will devour anyone they can without mercy.

The Scriptures, originally composed in Hebrew, were written from right to left. In contrast, our contemporary American culture follows a left-to-right writing system. However, it is important to recognize that God's perspective on the world and His Scriptures remains unchanged. To approach God, we must first acknowledge our sinful nature and our need for a Savior. True repentance involves ceasing from sin and submitting to the authority of Christ; only then are we eligible to receive His grace.

"Therefore I testify and protest to you on this [our parting] day that I am clean and innocent and not responsible for the blood of any of you. For I never shrank or kept back or fell short from declaring to you the whole purpose and plan and counsel of God. Take care and be on guard for yourselves and the whole flock over which the Holy Spirit has appointed you bishops and guardians, to shepherd (tend and feed and guide) the church of the Lord or

of God which He obtained for Himself [buying it and saving it for Himself] with His own blood" (Acts 20:26-28, Amplified).

I stand before you today with the same message Paul had for the early church. An adherence to the law is a requirement to continue in your salvation, but don't ever forget you were unworthy and in need of a Savior. It is not your works, but Jesus' sacrifice that atoned for your sins.

Left-handed demons want you to pervert the truth through inaccurate religion. They want you to misunderstand or misinterpret either the law or the grace of our God. As in Paul's day, these demons try to come into the Church without a strong shepherd and we must be on guard against them. Paul's admonition to the Ephesian church applies to us today:

"I know that after I am gone, ferocious wolves will get in among you, not sparing the flock; Even from among your own selves men will come to the front who, by saying perverse (distorted and corrupt) things, will endeavor to draw away the disciples after them [to their own party]. Therefore be always alert and on your guard, being mindful that for three years I never stopped night or day seriously to admonish and advise and exhort you one by one with tears. And now [brethren], I commit you to God [I deposit you in His charge, entrusting you to His protection and care]. And I commend you to the Word of His grace [to the commands and counsels and promises of His unmerited favor]. It is able to build you up and to give you [your rightful] inheritance among all God's set-apart ones (those consecrated, purified, and transformed of soul)" (Acts 20:29-32, Amplified).

9

The Degradation Spectrum

In our modern world, many people have become detached from the importance of a garden. Some even refrain from growing their own food because they can access fruits, vegetables, and other foods without needing to tend to a garden. However, throughout history gardens were incredibly important. In the past without a garden people would not have had food to eat.

Outside of most castles there are flourishing gardens. Kings and queens have never relied on the commoners to provide them with food. Royal families are totally self-sufficient and have their own garden, gardeners, and a system to attain healthy and whole food for their enjoyment. Kings have agricultural and culinary knowledge because they have people who work for them to ensure they eat the best of the land.

God's house is the most magnificent castle that exists. God is the highest ruling monarch. The Bible tells us the world is the Lord's footstool. This analogy tells us how small the world is in comparison to God and His kingdom:

"'Heaven is my throne, and the earth is my footstool. What kind of house will you build for me? says the Lord. Or where will my resting place be?" (Acts 7:49, NIV)

When envisioning mansions or castles, we often focus on their interiors; however, the exterior is equally significant. The gardens surrounding these grand structures are expansive and lush, featuring an array of greenery, including flowers, fruits, and vegetables. God's house is a mansion, and Jesus sits on a throne. The people of the world are part of His creation, but we are indeed a small part of it.

Isaiah 5:7 tells us, *"For the vineyard of the Lord of hosts is the house (nation) of Israel And the men of Judah are His delightful planting [which He loves]. So He looked for justice, but in fact, [He saw] bloodshed and lawlessness; [He looked] for righteousness, but in fact, [He heard] a cry of distress and oppression."* (AMPC)

Geographically, Israel is a small country compared to the rest of the countries of the world. Historically, vineyards would be placed beside the garden, because gardens were more inclusive incorporating other types of plants. If Israel is the Lord's vineyard and the rest of the world is grafted in through Christ, we are all apart of God's garden/vineyard, even though we are of different genders, cultures, races, or other varieties.

God lets us know we are all an essential part of the castle. Gender, race, culture, and other human qualities are simply representative of differences in expression, but children of God are a part of God's kingdom. When we are saved, we are members of the royal family. We are permitted into the castle and the surrounding areas. We are given special privileges. Each one of God's children are given an access key to the kingdom of God and its resources.

God does not give the keys for the rooms in His mansion to some and not to others. Romans 2:11 teaches, *"For God shows no partiality [no arbitrary favoritism; with Him one person is not more important than another]."* (AMPC) As a good Father, the King allows us all to eat at His table. He allows us to partake in the good things of the Holy Spirit as long as we are members of the family, and this permits us to thrive and grow supernaturally and abundantly.

Matthew 7:7-8 teaches us, *"Ask and it will be given to you; seek and you will find; knock and the door will be opened to you. For everyone who asks receives; the one who seeks finds; and to the one who knocks, the door will be opened."*

As God's children we are sent out on a mission to a lost and dying world, to retrieve more people and bring them into the safety of our castle walls to join our family, with supernatural assistance and backing from our King. We are duel citizens, representing heaven while living on the earth. The fruits we cultivate for God can be utilized to benefit those who need to be fed, hydrated, and restored back to life.

As we cultivate fruits for God, we naturally extend our support to those beyond His immediate family. God possesses an abundance of resources and sustenance, sufficient to care for His household as well as for all willing individuals in the surrounding area.

Consider Revelation 22:1-2: *"Then the angel showed me the river of the water of life, bright as crystal, flowing from the throne of God and of the Lamb through the middle of the street of the city; also, on either side of the river, the tree of life with its twelve kinds of fruit, yielding its fruit each month. The leaves of the tree were for the healing of the nations."* (ESV) Leaves are distinct from fruit. If the leaves of the tree of life can heal nations, envision how big just one tree in heaven is.

Fruit and leaves are distinct categories; however, they function together to support the plant's growth and benefit those who rely on it. Likewise, strawberries are not better than kiwis, and tulips are not better than daisies. Although different in color or size or other characteristics, all these creations have been intentionally crafted by a Creator for a purpose. All fruits, vegetables, and other plants were created to thrive and prosper while they are alive. As with these, God doesn't look at race, the gender, the socioeconomic position, or other appearances, to determine if we are "good or bad." He sees us as alive, or dead, fruitful, or unfruitful, and this is based on our relationship to Christ.

John 15:1-4 explains, *"I am the true vine, and my Father is the gardener. He cuts off every branch in me that bears no fruit, while every branch that does bear fruit he prunes so that it will be even more fruitful. You are already clean because of the word I have spoken to you. Remain in me, as I also remain in you. No branch can bear fruit by itself; it must remain in the vine. Neither can you bear fruit unless you remain in me."* (NIV)

Many castles would have had vineyards and gardens alongside one another. Each of these areas was distinctive, but they were both essential areas to the king. The choice to accept Jesus Christ as our Savior and the choice to remain in Him, walking in His ways, assures us we are a part of the vine and that we are going to thrive wherever we are. As Christians, regardless of our individual human expressions, we will thrive and prosper if we stay connected to Christ.

Women who keep Jesus Christ as their Head and their leader will dominate and thrive over men who are unsaved. They will also dominate and thrive over those both men and women who are saved but are lukewarm or lightly associated with Jesus, because Jesus Christ is the one who prospers and promotes. The distinction between male and female is not the defining factor of productivity. Rather, it is the quality of the vine, the availability of water, and the care provided by the gardener that ultimately determine success.

Jesus is the one who determines our path and gives us what we need to live as we focus on Him. Christians don't operate under the norms of the rest of society. We operate in a system completely outside of the secular world. We operate on a higher level within a higher dimension, because we are not of this world and neither is our Master.

Many cultures throughout history have been deceived by demons and allowed them to perpetrate the degradation of distinct groups. Demons want to destroy the order, and the categories God has made, and they want to separate through classification of people by groups in an unholy way. Satan tempts mankind to attribute value to groups by external characteristics such as gender, race, socioeconomic status, or other physical manifestations. He wants people to think they are valuable because of who they are as opposed to who God is.

Unlike Satan, God looks at the inner part of a person. He sees their heart and the faith, as opposed to their external state. God will prosper all who come to Him in faith. Second Kings 8:6 says, *"So the king appointed a certain officer for her saying, "Restore all that was hers, and all the proceeds of the field from the day that she left the land until now.""* God is a restorative God, who has *proven* **He is** willing to make anyone fruitful in an instant, when they are associated with Christ and have faith to come before Him.

Hebrews 4:16 teaches us, *"So let us come boldly to the throne of our gracious God. There we will receive his mercy, and we will find grace to help us when we need it most."* God is willing that none will perish and He will speak back to unbelievers who inquire of Him. How much more then will He speak and help His children from His own family and household?

First Timothy 5:8 explains, *"But those who won't care for their relatives, especially those in their own household, have denied the true faith. Such people are worse than unbelievers."*

When God separates families and people groups, He separates them to create order, not chaos. When God separates the wheat from the chaff, He protects the people who are in right standing with Him, and He keeps His Word to fulfill the covenants He has made with them.

First Kings 11:11-12 says, *"Therefore the Lord said to Solomon, "Because you have done this and have not kept My covenant and My statutes, which I have commanded you, I will certainly tear the kingdom away from you and give it to your servant. However, I will not do it in your lifetime, for the sake of your father David, but I will tear it out of the hand of your son (Rehoboam)."*

God is highly intelligent. He holds all wisdom and knowledge, and He is not ignorant of people's differences. Yet his criteria for assigning and separating them by groups is unlike our human groupings.

"So I ask, did they stumble in order that they might fall? By no means! Rather, through their trespass salvation has come to the Gentiles, so as to make Israel jealous. Now if their trespass means riches for the world, and if their failure means riches for the Gentiles, how much more will their full inclusion mean! Now I am speaking to you Gentiles. Inasmuch then as I am an apostle to the Gentiles, I magnify my ministry in order somehow to make my fellow Jews jealous, and thus save some of them. For if their rejection means the reconciliation of the world, what will their acceptance mean but life from the dead? If the dough offered as firstfruits is holy, so is the whole lump, and if the root is holy, so are the branches.

But if some of the branches were broken off, and you, although a wild olive shoot, were grafted in among the others and now share in the nourishing root of the olive tree, do not be arrogant toward the branches. If you are, remember it is not you who support the root, but the root that supports you. Then you will say, "Branches were broken off so that I might be grafted in." That is true. They were broken off because of their unbelief, but you stand fast through faith. So do not become proud, but fear. For if God did not spare the natural branches, neither will he spare you. Note then the kindness and the severity of God: severity toward those who have fallen, but God's kindness to you, provided you continue in his kindness. Otherwise you too will be cut off. And even they, if they do not continue in their unbelief, will be grafted in, for God has the power to graft them in again. For if you were cut from what is by nature a wild olive tree, and grafted, contrary to nature, into a cultivated olive tree, how much more will these, the natural branches, be grafted back into their own olive tree" (Romans 11:11-24, ESV).

To use the outward appearance to demean, degrade, or harm another person made in God's image, is to use Satan's measuring stick, not God's. Christian women who believe they are superior to men, or Christian men who believe they are superior to women, because of their blessing and their acceptance by God are in danger of being cut off. God makes it very plain that we are not to become proud, because being proud is a sin and a violation of God's standards for His people.

Proverbs 16:18 says, "*Pride goes before destruction, And a haughty spirit before a fall.*" (AMPC) A proud spirit is a spirit of rebellion. Satan's heart became proud, and he rebelled against God. The devil has created a spectrum of degradation, hoping Christians will fall into his trap so he can lure them away from God.

It is possible to be cut off from the Lord and lose your place in God's Garden and vineyard because you exalt yourself and your unique characteristics, instead of humbling yourself and being thankful for the position given to you by God. Satan once held an important role and position in God's house. He had the luxuries and the lifestyle of a prince, but he forfeited it due to his rebellion and ambition for more. Isaiah 14:2 explains, *"How you have fallen from heaven,morning star, son of the dawn!You have been cast down to the earth,you who once laid low the nations! "*

Let's return to the story in Esther for a moment. King Xerxes, in his embellishment and his proud heart, determined to have a banquet and a party in the palace to show off the things he possessed. The king had men of various rankings and positions at the banquet, and the men were indulging in their flesh and having as much wine as they desired.

"In the third year of his reign he made a feast for all his princes and his courtiers. The chief officers of the Persian and Median army and the nobles and governors of the provinces were there before him. While he showed the riches of his glorious kingdom and the splendor and excellence of his majesty for many days, even 180 days. And when these days were completed, the king made a feast for all the people present in Shushan the capital, both great and small, a seven-day feast in the court of the garden of the king's palace. There were hangings of fine white cloth, of green and of blue [cotton], fastened with cords of fine linen and purple to silver rings or rods and marble pillars. The couches of gold and silver rested on a [mosaic] pavement of porphyry, white marble, mother-of-pearl, and [precious] colored stones. Drinks were served in different kinds of golden goblets, and there was royal wine in abundance, according to the liberality of the king. And drinking was according to the law;

no one was compelled to drink, for the king had directed all the officials of his palace to serve only as each guest desired. Also Queen Vashti gave a banquet for the women in the royal house which belonged to King Ahasuerus" (Esther 1:1-9, Amplified).

In this story, the men and the women were distinctively separated for their banquets. They were not mixed, as they were seen as unique groups, with Queen Vashti leading the women and King Xerxes leading the men. This illustrates that when God created man and the woman, He made them to be unique and separate in His house. He made them operate in their own distinctive ways, both valuable and important but different in their characteristics and functions. Men are not women, and women are not men, but both are permitted to enjoy the luxuries of the King's house.

King Xerxes, in his folly determined he was going to go against the appropriate cultural standards and invite a woman, Queen Vashti, into the company of the men. His motivation was pride, where he could present her as another object to possess and enjoy, instead of a person to value and respect. King Xerxes' command was in opposition to God's design, because women were not to join the company of men and act like a man, and they were not created to be used and abused as an object for man's personal gratification and enjoyment.

"On the seventh day, when the king's heart was merry with wine, he commanded Mehuman, Biztha, Harbona, Bigtha, Abagtha, Zethar, and Carkas, the seven eunuchs who ministered to King Ahasuerus as attendants, To bring Queen Vashti before the king, with her royal crown, to show the peoples and the princes her beauty, for she was fair to behold. But Queen Vashti refused to come at the king's command conveyed by the eunuchs. Therefore the king was enraged, and his anger burned within him" (Esther 1:10-13, Amplified).

The eunuchs were permitted to go between the men and the women alike because they were neutered and their gender was nonexistent. These men were castrated so they would be "gender neutral," or fluid, exerting no male or female sexual desires or characteristics.

Demons and angels alike do not have gender because they were made to be messengers between the king and the people.

In Matthew 22:30 Jesus gives further explanation on this subject: *"For in the resurrection neither do men marry nor are women given in marriage, but they are like angels in heaven [who do not marry nor produce children]."* (AMPC) It is for this reason that demons want to cause gender confusion and transgenderism within humans. Demons want humans to look and act like them, not like God's design for men and women. So they tempt humans to distort and destroy the distinct categories of gender.

Operating under a demon spirit of alcohol, King Xerxes became confused about gender roles and gender distinctions. He began to blur the gender lines, and he unjustly dominated a female using his authority to perform evil as opposed to good, based on his gender. This illustrates that demons hate the distinctions and intentional design of a man and woman and hate that the Lord created both groups to dine and enjoy the best of His house. They continue to go about today on a mission to destroy the lines of gender and to use gender as a means of violence against anyone they can.

Men either within the Church or in the world who feel superior to women are under the influence of a demonic spirit. When men use their gender and sexual anatomy as a tool of violence, they are working for Satan. In God's kingdom, women have their unique functions, but we eat in pleasure in our own banquet rooms. We are separate from men but not inferior, and we are not to be abused and treated as objects to use only for the men's enjoyment.

Women are not denied access to the good of the land because we are women. God has a special place for us, where we can share in the Holy Spirit and the gifts of the Spirit, apart from the men in our own banquet rooms. Women are chosen, used by God, and anointed. We are permitted access into the King's house, and we are given weapons to destroy the works of our enemy because God loves us and has called us to be a part of His family.

Abuse of women by men is on one end of the degradation spectrum. This demonic spirit leads men to falsely assume superiority and to discredit and abuse the women of the house. Through an authoritarian leadership style, men under the sway of this demonic influence will use strict rules, high standards, and punishment to harm women. They will not be flexible, understanding, compassionate, or caring toward women. Instead, they will harm women and trivialize their humanity because they feel they are superior to them.

This abuse of women is, at its core, the worship of man. And the worship of the male anatomy and the belief that men are better than women is from hell. No one whether they are a man or woman should worship the created being of man/woman. Idolizing and exalting oneself because of gender assigned by God at birth, is one of the modern-day exhibitions of pride where one believes they are elevated simply because of who they are.

On the other side of the spectrum is a demon spirit that wants to lure women into the same falsehood. This is the feminist spirit, as we covered in a previous chapter. It promises women freedom from their mistreatment at the hands of men. By worshiping the female instead of the male, women follow feminism into a very similar place. Where the women deceived by this spirit worship the woman, as opposed to the man.

Women who have been abused and mistreated are more likely to be prey to this demon spirit because it will manifest and promise the woman a better life, if they submit and follow it. But we must know demon spirits operate to get us to bow, just once so they can dominate our lives. The demon spirits never do what they promise, and if we follow them, we will always end up worse off than we were before.

First Peter 2:22-23 says, *He committed no sin, nor was deceit ever found in his mouth. While being reviled and insulted, He did not revile or insult in return; while suffering, He made no threats [of vengeance], but kept entrusting Himself to Him who judges fairly.* (AMPC)

Women who want to be like Christ must resist the spirit of feminism so they can remain free from the entrapment of the devil. When Jesus was abused and reviled and insulted, He didn't respond through aggression and personal vengeance. Jesus put all things into the hands of His Father, and He continued His mission. As we choose to resist the feminist spirit, we can know the Father and fair Judge in heaven sees all things and wants us to present our case to Him.

Christians have a duty to ensure we are never at the extreme end of either of these ideologies. We must remain awake and diligent, guarding our hearts, as it is possible to become completely numb and disconnected from either side, choosing to hold no claims on gender, and this is also demonic. To walk in truth, we must remain in our distinct places, as male and female, and we must hold onto the unique and equal rights of both groups.

Proverbs 31:1-9 teaches, *"The words of King Lemuel. An oracle that his mother taught him: What are you doing, my son? What are you doing, son of my womb? What are you doing, son of my vows? Do not give your strength to women, your ways to those who destroy kings. It is not for kings, O Lemuel, it is not for kings to drink wine, or for rulers to take strong drink, lest they drink and forget what has been decreed and pervert the rights of all the afflicted. Give strong drink to the one who is perishing, and wine to those in bitter distress; let them drink and forget their poverty and remember their misery no more. Open your mouth for the mute, for the rights of all who are destitute. Open your mouth, judge righteously, defend the rights of the poor and needy."* (ESV)

God wants us to open our mouths wide for the rights of the marginalized and the abused. He wants us to stand up for the people in distress and those who are being held captive by a mute spirit and can't speak up for themselves. A subgroup of demonic spirits works overtime to silence people. And they particularly want to gag and keep the voices of God's people from going forth into the world.

In His ministry, Jesus silenced demons, and he healed people from mute spirits. Jesus hated the devils speaking, but He permitted men, women, and children to speak freely. Luke 4:35 explains, *"But Jesus re-buked him, saying, "Be silent (muzzled, gagged) and come out of him!" And when the demon had thrown the man down among them, he came out of him without injuring him in any way."* (AMPC)

A mute spirit's objective is to stop people from communicating. Women throughout history have been marginalized, abused, and si-lenced by evil men. Demonically inspired men have done everything possible to allow Satan to bind and silence innocent women. How-ever, today we see the feminist spirit trying to silence men, alongside of the domineering abusive male spirit trying to silence women. Fem-inist women want men's voices eradicated. They want men to be in-timidated to speak against them.

Mute spirits will stop at nothing to silence the voices of the saints, and we must ensure we never allow them to silence us and stop us from proclaiming the truth! Men, women, and children must rise in the anointing and speak the truth of God's word freely. If you have been struggling to speak freely for the Lord, God wants you to be free. Jesus Christ died for us to use our authority against Satan, and a part of our authority is the right to speak and command the evil spirits to shut up, so we are permitted to speak instead.

Notice this story in Mark 9:22-25: *"The demon has often thrown him both into fire and into water, intending to kill him. But if You can do any-thing, take pity on us and help us!" Jesus said to him, "[You say to Me,] 'If You can?' All things are possible for the one who believes and trusts [in Me]!" Immediately the father of the boy cried out [with a desperate, piercing cry], saying, "I do believe; help [me overcome] my unbelief." When Jesus saw that a crowd was rapidly gathering [around them], He rebuked the unclean spirit, saying to it, "You deaf and mute spirit, I command you, come out of him and never enter him again!""* (AMPC)

Now, I take my authority in Christ Jesus, and I bind any mute spirit operating in the lives of anyone who is reading this book. God's people will speak without demonic interference from this day for-ward. We will use our voice to proclaim the truth, regardless of who likes it. As people created in the image of God, we were created to speak the Word and use it as a weapon against Satan and as a medicine for the people of the world. We will fulfill our call and our mission. We cannot be stopped.

Today, many women face banishment, abuse, and unjust punishment within their places of worship due to their refusal to accept a subordinate status. Much like the "separate but equal" laws in the United States, women recognize the inequity in their treatment, despite being told otherwise. But let our refusal to participate in their banquet serve as a powerful reminder to those who perpetuate injustice that we will not yield or relinquish our God-given rights.

It is always the righteous thing to stand up against evil. As we stand for women's voices in the Church, we know God stands with us because we are on the side of truth and justice. Banishment and harsh punishments towards women are recorded in heaven. God sees the mistreatment of His daughters, and we can choose today to entrust our abuse to the Judge who judges fairly. And in the meantime, we can speak boldly for the truth and do our part to free the people who want to be set free.

Paul warns, *Do not repay anyone evil for evil. Be careful to do what is right in the eyes of everyone. If it is possible, as far as it depends on you, live at peace with everyone. Do not take revenge, my dear friends, but leave room for God's wrath, for it is written: "It is mine to avenge; I will repay," says the Lord* (Romans 12:17-19, NIV).

When we stand for the truth in a godly way, we aren't using another unholy doctrine to fight evil. Fighting evil with evil will never work. Standing for the rights of others in righteousness and truth, and permitting God to help us, is not the same as ascribing ourselves to a doctrine such as feminism. We must choose to remain pure and loving toward all men, even when we must stand against the injustice and the corruption concurrently.

Queen Vashti's holy resistance to the devil was used by the Lord because God made room for Esther through the refusal to bow to an unholy king. Vashti provoked the king, inciting his wrath—a reaction often associated with the devil when he is not honored. By defying expectations, Vashti thwarted the devil's schemes and prevented malevolence from infiltrating the palace.

"According to law, what must be done to Queen Vashti?" he asked. "She has not obeyed the command of King Xerxes that the eunuchs have taken to her" (Esther 1:15, Amplified).

The evil men in the leadership positions were bothered by her refusal, and this shows us the devil's empire was disrupted. Vashti was living in a self-controlled, self-denial manner. She was willing to keep the order God had established separating the men and the women. Her beauty was internal, not external and she refused to be objectified by the king, even though he was her husband. If a woman can do the work of the Lord setting the stage for the salvation of the Jews, by refusing to be abused by a man, while advocating for the distinct roles of gender, we can too!

As we choose to love our womanhood and stand proudly in our distinct and valuable roles in our King's house, we will take ground from the enemy and disrupt his agendas. Our hearts will remain pure as opposed to being proud. We are not better or worse than the men in God's house. We are distinct and we are to be different, but we are not more valuable or less valuable because of our external characteristics.

God's family and His garden is filled with diversity. The King's palace and garden surpasses anything we could envision. In His eyes, there is no distinction of worth among us; He does not judge based on appearance. Instead, God examines the heart, focusing on the intrinsic qualities of each person—their character and values. The inner essence ultimately determines whether one will continue to flourish or be severed from the vine.

We must never become proud because of the position God has given us. This proud and haughty spirit dear friends, was the sole thing behind Satan's rebellion. A beautiful angel, a special part of God's kingdom, ruined and destroyed for an eternity, because he believed he was better than he was, thinking he alone was permitted to rule and to reign over all of the other things and creations that God made.

The Church is not going to be distracted from building for the Lord and doing the work of God. We will not stop the work God has for us because we are worried about gender ideologies. Everyone has a job to do, but we are all on the same team, working for the King of Kings and the Lord of Lords. Let us rejoice today that we are eligible to do this great work. I am thankful we have been granted access into the greatest place existing either on the heaven or on the earth, and I pray I will never become arrogant, proud, and unthankful, or submit to an antichrist spirit of self-indulgence and pride. Will you pray the same?

So built we the wall; and all the wall was joined together unto the half thereof: for the people had a mind to work. But it came to pass, that when Sanballat, and Tobiah, and the Arabians, and the Ammonites, and the Ashdodites, heard that the walls of Jerusalem were made up, and that the breaches began to be stopped, then they were very wroth, And conspired all of them together to come and to fight against Jerusalem, and to hinder it. Nevertheless we made our prayer unto our God, and set a watch against them day and night, because of them. And Judah said, The strength of the bearers of burdens is decayed, and there is much rubbish; so that we are not able to build the wall. And our adversaries said, They shall not know, neither see, till we come in the midst among them, and slay them, and cause the work to cease. And it came to pass, that when the Jews which dwelt by them came, they said unto us ten times, From all places whence ye shall return unto us they will be upon you. Therefore set I in the lower places behind the wall, and on the higher places, I even set the people after their families with their swords, their spears, and their bows. And I looked, and rose up, and said unto the nobles, and to the rulers, and to the rest of the people, Be not ye afraid of them: remember the Lord, which is great and terrible, and fight for your brethren, your sons, and your daughters, your wives, and your houses. And it came to pass, when our enemies heard that it was known unto us, and God had brought their counsel to nought, that we returned all of us to the wall, every one unto his work (Nehemiah 4:1-15).

10

The Vengeance of the Lord

Throughout the ages, people have loved entertainment. Before televisions, radio, and other modern technologies, people, especially the wealthy, would hire entertainers such as musicians, jugglers, snake charmers, and storytellers to entertain them with their performances.

By occupation, minstrels/jesters, also called fools, would work in the palace courts, in towns, and on battlefields executing their duties in an allegiance to the ruler they served through their public performance. Jesters did not always wear a silly hat and outfit, even though they were known to do ridiculous things to make people laugh.

Jesters brought comic relief to serious and lighthearted situations, and they brought ease to people even during challenging times. Being a jester/fool was often an honorable position. Most were permitted close access to the king and lived elegant and affluent lifestyles.

One of the primary jobs of jesters was performing in front of audiences, as well as relaying important or sensitive information that would sometimes go to the people, the armies of the enemy or the king, and to the king himself. When not performing, jesters were tasked with revealing information, good and bad, and finding ways to reveal that information to others.

Jesters still exist in the spiritual realm with the spiritual world full of rulers. These men and women dance, sing, and perform, and they send messages both to people and opposing forces.

In societies throughout history, occupations were decided by the family you were born into. The last name of the family and the occupation of the family were telling signs of the occupation of the young man or woman born into the family. In Nehemiah we are told each family, according to their name and specific work, did the jobs they were commanded to do.

Family name and the relationship to occupation is why people called Jesus the son of the carpenter:—*"Is this not the carpenter, the son of Mary, and the brother of James and Joses and Judas and Simon? Are His sisters not here with us?" And they were [deeply] offended by Him [and their disapproval blinded them to the fact that He was anointed by God as the Messiah]"* (Mark 6:3, Amplified).

Jesters were unique in their occupational origins because they did not have to come from a certain family of origin. They could come from a variety of backgrounds and family systems. The primary qualifications of a successful jester was not their family lineage but their talents. If a jester was pleasing to a ruler, they would be taken in by the ruler and given a job.

In the spiritual realm, jesters are those who have a prophetic gift. Singers and songwriters, writers, artists, actors, and comedians are some of the trades of jesters. People who are called to the arts and to a life of performance and entertainment are the people who please or displease the rulers in the Spirit. Men and women with prophetic gifts are going to be entertaining, pleasing, and serving someone, but the question is whom?

As in the past with royalty, the wealthy and the world leaders, both physically and spiritually, call the shots for the entertainment industry. This phenomenon is spiritual, and unless it is dealt with through the realm of the Spirit, it cannot be dealt with at all.

Paul reminds us, *"For our struggle is not against flesh and blood [contending only with physical opponents], but against the rulers, against the powers, against the world forces of this [present] darkness, against the spiritual forces of wickedness in the heavenly (supernatural) places"* (Ephesians 6:12, Amplified).

The rise and the fall of the jester throughout history was determined through their ability to keep their ruler happy and entertained. When the jester failed in this mission, they were often killed or thrown out of their jobs. The rulers who influence the spirit world today will find prophetic people they can work through to control as their personal jesters. These rulers find jesters who are willing to sing, dance, speak, draw, and write for them, entertaining them and their society at large.

The spiritual war we are in is the precise reason the entertainment industry is so demonic and polluted with filth. There are demons behind the individuals in high places, and these demons find entertainers to partner with them to entertain the masses, to send messages to the enemy forces, and to entertain the affluent men and women. Prophetic people need to be warned and aware of the people who will try to traffic and pollute their gift. A prophetic gift can be used for God or another spirit ready to distort the gift.

Jesters who failed to please a ruler often became beggars and homeless. Today, we see this same pattern happening to artists and those who have a prophetic call and don't please a high-ranking ruler. A jester who fails to please a ruler in the high places, lives a vagabond life, wandering from place to place, with no headship. Many people with prophetic gifts are homeless or close to it if they have not done anything to please a ruler in the realm of the spirit.

All rulers are either good or evil. Some kings, queens, and rulers in history were ruthless and cutthroat, and others were caring and just. Satan is a coldblooded ruler, and other heartless demonic rulers work beneath him in high places. In the book of Daniel, we are told of the prince of Persia, in the realm of the spirit, and this spirit kept Daniel from receiving his answer for a short time. This prince was a ruler working in an area or principality.

"Then he said to me, "Do not be afraid, Daniel, for from the first day that you set your heart on understanding this and on humbling yourself before your God, your words were heard, and I have come in response to your words. But the prince of the kingdom of Persia was standing in opposition to me for twenty-one days. Then, behold, Michael, one of the chief [of the celestial] princes, came to help me, for I had been left there with the kings of Persia" (Daniel 10:12-13, Amplified).

Daniel pleased God and refused to bow to the unholy spirits. Demon spirits want us to bow to them just once so they can take dominion over our lives. When the demon spirits through King Xerxes asked Queen Vashti to submit, it was one time. When the devil tempted Jesus in the desert, he wanted Him to bow to him only once.

We see throughout scripture that Satan and the demonic realm desire compromise, even just once. Imagine if Daniel, Shadrach, Meshach, and Abednego had been willing to compromise, even just once. They would have been under the domination of the devil instead of being a light for God. One submission to evil and idols would have kept us from knowing their stories.

Our choice to never bow to the Antichrist Spirit or the lesser ruling demonic spirits roaming the earth matters. Prophetic people who refuse to work for the demonic realm will be rewarded. Remaining faithful and holy before the Lord is a protection for our lives. If we want to increase and we want to take ground from the enemy, we must be willing to do what these courageous men and women did and say no every single time we are presented with an option to bow.

"Son of man, say to the prince of Tyre, Thus says the Lord God: Because your heart is lifted up and you have said and thought, I am a god, I sit in the seat of the gods, in the heart of the seas; yet you are only man [weak, feeble, made of earth] and not God, though you imagine yourself to be almost more than mortal with your mind as the mind of God; Indeed, you are [imagining yourself] wiser than Daniel; there is no secret [you think] that is

hidden from you; With your own wisdom and with your own understanding you have gotten you riches and power and have brought gold and silver into your treasuries; By your great wisdom and by your traffic you have increased your riches and power, and your heart is proud and lifted up because of your wealth" (Ezekiel 28:1-5, Amplified).

The prince of Tyre was proud, believing in his heart he was more important than he was. He was a rich, important leader in the land, but he was detested by the Lord because his heart was proud. Satan is behind all forms of pride and self-esteem. He is the enslaver of humanity, masquerading as a provider of freedom and pleasure. Satan both entraps and exploits individuals, perpetuating a cycle of enslavement that ensnares others as well.

The devil is the ruler over all the other demonic leaders and rulers. He is the head over all the ranks of devils. Satan is pictured as a king ruler in Scripture, and in the book of Ezekiel we are told he is behind all trafficking on the earth. Satan is the original musical being, once beautiful, anointed, and worthy to the highest King. But once he became proud and believed he was superior to his King, he became the first to traffic/pimp out the anointing.

"Son of man, take up a lamentation over the king of Tyre and say to him, Thus says the Lord God: You are the full measure and pattern of exactness [giving the finishing touch to all that constitutes completeness], full of wisdom and perfect in beauty. You were in Eden, the garden of God; every precious stone was your covering, the carnelian, topaz, jasper, chrysolite, beryl, onyx, sapphire, carbuncle, and emerald; and your settings and your sockets and engravings were wrought in gold. On the day that you were created they were prepared.

You were the anointed cherub that covers with overshadowing [wings], and I set you so. You were upon the holy mountain of God; you walked up and down in the midst of the stones of fire [like the paved work of gleaming sapphire stone upon which the God of Israel walked on Mount Sinai]. You were blameless in your ways from the day you were created until iniquity and guilt were found in you.

*Through the abundance of your commerce you were filled with lawless-
ness and violence, and you sinned; therefore I cast you out as a profane thing
from the mountain of God and the guardian cherub drove you out from the
midst of the stones of fire. Your heart was proud and lifted up because of your
beauty; you corrupted your wisdom for the sake of your splendor. I cast you
to the ground; I lay you before kings, that they might gaze at you.*

*You have profaned your sanctuaries by the multitude of your iniquities
and the enormity of your guilt, by the unrighteousness of your trade. Therefore I have brought forth a fire from your midst; it has consumed you, and
I have reduced you to ashes upon the earth in the sight of all who looked at
you. All who know you among the people are astonished and appalled at you;
you have come to a horrible end and shall never return to being"* (Ezekiel 28,
Amplified).

Many entertainers are deceived and proud as the devil was. They
begin to believe the gifts God has given them and their talents are
their own to use as they please. Because of their beauty and special
calling, many entertainers are prey to the devil, because he often understands their call better than they do. When Satan sees young talent, he will target the man or the woman and he will offer them a deal,
a commerce arrangement, so he can benefit and enjoy personally and
publicly the talent of the man or woman.

Like a pimp who sees a young girl, Satan offers the individual help,
protection, and financial support. Satan will pretend to be on the en-
tertainer's side, helping and exalting them to a high place when he
intends to demean, control, and degrade the person under his domination. Many women who have a prophetic gift also become prey to
sex work, such as prostitution, stripping or pornographic movies. The
same devil uses the beauty and prophetic call of the woman to lure her
into a high place of public humiliation for his kingdom's benefit and
financial profit.

As in the days of old, most entertainers today live in luxury because of their association with a demon ruler. Financial gain, pop-
ularity and the chance to speak to the masses of people are perks

associated with the job of a jester. However, jesters have historically been expected to demonstrate unwavering loyalty and obedience to their rulers. Those who refuse to comply often face dire consequences, including execution or expulsion from their roles, relegating them to a lower status within society.

Jesters notoriously have been killed by their rulers or the enemy forces. Many jesters were murdered by those within their own camp. When we see young entertainers abruptly killed and destroyed for failure to go along with the system, we are seeing publicly the murder of a displeasing jester. Jesters are spectacles to society. They are watched by the people around them, and they are exalted so they can please their ruler.

Satan wants people to worship him instead of worshiping God. He wants to use jesters as voices to the masses so he can entertain and prophetically influence large groups of people. When a prophet, good or evil, uses their gift to speak, write, act, or perform for others, their actions, words, and behavior have an impact on anyone who witnesses and believes/internalizes the message sent out. It is a proven fact that music, books, and other forms of entertainment are prophetically used to change the trajectory of people's lives through spiritual power.

If humans are not serving the Lord, they are still serving, but they are serving a much harsher, and inferior, master. We will serve God or Satan. Prophetic gifts will be used, and if they aren't used for good, Satan will pollute them and use them for evil. God did not create either the man or woman to serve themselves. When God made us, He made us to serve Him and to help edify others through our talents and gifts.

Jesus, God's Son with high esteem and authority, gave His life for others to thrive and succeed. If we serve Him, we will succeed, but we won't suffer alongside it. Unlike the devil, God will prosper us and work with us, and He will give us a thriving and happy life, with no torment or sorrow.

As we use our gifts for God, we will live lives of luxury, and we will be loved and respected, underneath the headship of an honorable, loving King, we will be taken care of and never lack anything. Psalm 34:10 explains, "*The young lions lack food and suffer hunger, but they who seek (inquire of and require) the Lord [by right of their need and on the authority of His Word], none of them shall lack any beneficial thing.*" (AMPC)

Wherever we start we can be more and be elevated to a higher place, through faith and obedience to God. If we are envious of others because they appear to be given closer access to God, it's not because of God's favoritism but because of the person's work, willingness, and obedience. When we please the King with our actions of faith, we are going to be brought before Him. If we want more from God, we must pursue Him, and when we do, we will find Him.

David was a regular boy in his society, and his decision to go after a giant caused him to be brought before the king. Proverbs 18:16 says, "*A man's gift [given in love or courtesy] makes room for him And brings him before great men.*" (AMPC)

David was a spiritual jester, and he was a man who brought pleasure to God, the King of the world. As David pleased God, he was brought before great men on the earth. David is well known for his musical talents, singing and dancing, and writing poetry. This prophetic gift was pure, and it was used for the kingdom of God, so his ruler eventually exalted him to the highest place on the earth: kingship.

As David continued to please God, enemies and common people knew his name. He was in a high place of society both politically and financially. He was famous.

Men and women with a prophetic gift will oftentimes be asked to do things that seem odd to the carnal mind, but when these acts are done in faith and obedience to God, He can use their lives as artwork and entertainment in front of all other people. Operating under a prophetic gift that pleases the Lord is assured to put us before men and women as an example, a witness, and a leader to others.

Prophets were often known to do some unconventional things. Consider Ezekiel, who was told by God to not mourn the death of his wife before the people. God wanted to use the life of Ezekiel and his actions to teach and represent His kingdom.

In the same way, prophetic people receive messages from the King directly, and take these messages to the people of society, prophets also carry messages to the enemies' camp, through charades and art, ensuring the enemy sees it and receives the message.

Moses, a prophet, was a "snake charmer." He went before the ruler in Egypt in demonstration of God's power. He displayed the reality of God and His truths through his performance. As actors on God's stage, prophets ensure that the enemies and the people receive the message from God. They convey the message of heaven, and they please God when they do their job well! The prophetic gift is an honorable gift, and it is a great blessing from the Lord.

"Now, the Lord's Spirit had left Saul, and an evil spirit from the Lord tormented him. Saul's officials told him, "An evil spirit from God is tormenting you. Your Majesty, why don't you command us to look for a man who can play the lyre well? When the evil spirit from God comes to you, he'll strum a tune, and you'll feel better." Saul told his officials, "Please find me a man who can play well and bring him to me." One of the officials said, "I know one of Jesse's sons from Bethlehem who can play well.

He's a courageous man and a warrior. He has a way with words, he is handsome, and the Lord is with him." Saul sent messengers to Jesse to say, "Send me your son David, who is with the sheep." Jesse took six bushels of bread, a full wineskin, and a young goat and sent them with his son David to Saul. David came to Saul and served him. Saul loved him very much and made David his armorbearer. Saul sent this message to Jesse, "Please let David stay with me because I have grown fond of him." Whenever God's spirit came to Saul, David took the lyre and strummed a tune. Saul got relief from his terror and felt better, and the evil spirit left him" (First Samuel 16:14-23, Amplified).

King Saul's torment was not a result of divine hatred; rather, it stemmed from his refusal to submit to God's authority leaving him vulnerable to the demonic. Men and women who submit to demon spirits will be tormented by them as Saul was. Many in the entertainment industry are in a continual state of unrest because of their association with the demonic. The choice to bow to the devil and his companions is traumatic for the person because demon spirits bring forth torture day and night.

11

Leadership, Dominion, & Appraisal

God is the only One who can protect us in the world we live in. Without God, we cannot defend ourselves from the evil trying to destroy us. From our childhood onward, we need protection. This is critical because demon spirits roam the earth looking for the vulnerable and weak. They look for people who are not living under the protection of God.

Our salvation and covenant with God through the blood sacrifice of Jesus Christ is our spiritual armor. The Lamb of God's blood on the doorpost of our house and spiritual bodies is our only hope against the forces of evil! Many people are unaware that they possess the ability to combat Satan in their life. Yet, it is vital to recognize that we have been equipped with the necessary tools to triumph against Satan. We are fully capable of overcoming various forms of attack, if we stand firm as believers.

Daily we are given a chance to take up our cross, show ourselves approved, and walk in faith. Jesus told the cripple man to "pick up his mat and walk." To receive God's victory in our lives, we must harness our faith and take consistent action.

First Timothy 6:12 says, *"Fight the good fight of the faith [in the conflict with evil]; take hold of the eternal life to which you were called, and [for which] you made the good confession [of faith] in the presence of many witnesses"*(AMPC)

In a good fight both parties are contending to win. The desire to win a fight fundamentally alters the level of engagement. Many Christians wrongfully take a passive approach in life and unfortunately this often translates into their battle with Satan. By believing the lie that Christians should embody passivity, weakness, and unconditional compassion towards all beings and circumstances, many inadvertently provide Satan with an advantage in the spiritual struggle.

Christians should not adopt a passive, weak, and ineffective stance in their relationships with others or with spiritual entities. Christians are called to assert themselves and stand firm in every circumstance, fully equipped with their supernatural guidance and wisdom from heaven. Born again Christians are rulers on the earth. We are the authority of Christ.

Deuteronomy 28:13 says, *"And the Lord will make you the head and not the tail, and you shall only go up and not down,"* (AMPC).

Opposing those who are agents of Satan is not a sin. In fact, standing up for our God and for ourselves as an ambassador in His kingdom is one of the most noble and honorable actions we can undertake, as it reflects our commitment to God and His kingdom, rather than our commitment to the world.

God wants us to have a high opinion of ourselves in Him. He commands us to approach self-assessment with clarity and honesty, so we can carry an accurate appraisal of our worth—neither inflated nor minimized. Romans 12:3 explains, *"For by the grace given me I say to every one of you: Do not think of yourself more highly than you ought, but rather think of yourself with sober judgment, in accordance with the faith God has distributed to each of you."*

Appraisal is a process of assessment. In an appraisal someone or something is examined and analyzed so a determination of it's worth can be discovered. As we appraise ourselves, we must realize we are very valuable and important to God and the kingdom of heaven. We must also understand the power of our faith as a tool and a weapon, so we can utilize what God has given us to perform His purposes for the earth.

Dominion and jurisdiction is apart of the covenant we have with God. The word dominion in Hebrew is *radah* which means to rule, tread, or govern. Time and time again throughout the Scriptures the Lord shows us and tells us about our ability to rule as His people. Ruling and controlling our lives, our families, our communities, and our world is one of the greatest blessings God has gifted us with as a Christian.

Until you can see yourself as God sees you, as a ruler and a leader in your family, your society, and within the world you will not take your proper authority position. God has appraised His people as rulers and leaders. He has told us our value in the world, but Satan works to undermine that appraisal. He wants to devalue us and create feelings of inferiority and servitude because this is the only chance he has for us to not overtake him and trump over his entire army and mission.

When a Christian is being harassed, harmed, or even threatened they should never stand idle and permit abusive treatment. Engaging boldly within the conflict and standing up for oneself exemplifies an understanding of proper appraisal and thus it demonstrates proper respect. It also shows the losing side who holds the power and the weakness they have. Being bold in Christ is distinct from pride; which is rooted in oneself outside of Christ.

Christians have dominion and with it we can refuse to allow the enemy to dictate the terms of our lives or the lives of others. Christians are not below Satan, he is below us. Even if it looks like, or feels like you have been knocked down, you should get back up and keep contending to win the fight. Our battle isn't over until God wins. Being knocked down doesn't mean you will lose a battle; it just means you are in a fight.

"The mouth of the righteous speaks wisdom, and his tongue talks of justice. The law of his God is in his heart; none of his steps shall slide. The wicked watches the righteous, And seeks to slay him. The Lord will not leave him in his hand. Nor condem him when he's judged. Wait on the Lord and keep his way. And He shall exalt you to inherit the land; when the wicked are cut off you shall see it. I have seen the wicked in great power, and spreading himself like a native green tree . Yet he passed again and behold he was no more. Indeed I sought him, but he could not be found.

Mark the blameless man and observe the upright; for the future of that man is peace. But the transgressors shall be destroyed together; The future of the wicked shall be cut off. But the salvation of the righteous is from the Lord; He is their strength in time of trouble And the Lord shall help them and deliver them, He shall deliver them from the wicked, And save them, Because they trust in Him" (Psalm 37:30-40, NKJV).

The adversary will continue to persist in his efforts to confront and undermine those who do not resist him, as he recognizes his advantageous position in seeking to overpower them. Without a proper mental stance of victory in Christ, the devil will trample over you even when God didn't intend for him to.

The Bible commands us to take up our shield of faith and resist Satan and his tactics. God tells us to never give into evil; because we were born again as new creatures so we could overcome evil. Romans 12:21 is one of my personal favorite scriptures because it tells us we aren't passive victims, instead we are powerful agents of change : *"Do not be overcome and conquered by evil, but overcome evil with good."* (AMPC)

Standing firm against evil is a conscious choice, one that involves rejecting any attempts at intimidation or domination by demonic forces. However, many people do not make this choice, because they do not seek refuge in the sacred connection with God. Psalm 91:1 explains, *"Whoever dwells in the shelter of the Most High will rest in the shadow of the Almighty."* (NIV)

To dwell means to live in. Living in unity and closeness with the Lord offers protection. It provides clarity in distinguishing right from wrong and safeguards us from missteps in life. By dwelling in the presence of God, we gain insight into our true selves and recognize the inherent value we possess, therefore we are empowered to navigate our human affairs with purpose and authority.

Praying one time or hearing God's voice one time is not sufficient for protection and strength against Satan. Faith in God and His Word is a lifestyle that involves a continual pressing into the things of the Lord. To live a life of victory, we need daily bread, daily provision, and daily communion with God.

The devil begins looking for his prey from childhood. This happened in Jesus' ministry on the earth where a boy was possessed by an evil spirit in his childhood. *"It has often thrown him into fire or water to kill him. But if you can do anything, take pity on us and help us"* (Mark 9:22, NIV).

Those who have become accustomed to being victimized by demons, people, or situations, have a much easier time taking on this identity but they will only become weaker, if they do not unlock God's deliverance. The boy's father in Mark 9 had enough faith in Jesus and His ministry to inquire His help. He realized there was a problem and he was willing to find the solution.

Adults need to take responsibility for their children, and adults must also take responsibility for their personal lives. Anyone who comes to Jesus can be saved, delivered, and set free. Anyone can be released from bondage and torment, but they must want it and come to Christ. As it is only after we have been rescued that we can choose to stand our ground and confront the enemy boldly and confidently.

Every time a Christian stands up to the bully Satan, he gets weaker, not us! When we resist him, rebuke him, and cast him out, he loses all of his power. The devil will flee and give up after he realizes he is fighting with someone who is anointed and refuses to quit the fight. The devil knows who carries the power of God and who doesn't.

Human bullies continue to target individuals who are unlikely to retaliate, often preying on those who are emotionally vulnerable. They have an ability to identify those who will continue to endure their aggression, exploiting this knowledge to perpetuate their bullying behavior. Like the human bullies who can smell emotional vulnerability, demons know who will and who won't challenge them and stop them.

Acts 19:16 says, *"Then some of the traveling Jewish exorcists also attempted to call the name of the Lord Jesus over those who had evil spirits, saying, "I implore you and solemnly command you by the Jesus whom Paul preaches!" Seven sons of one [named] Sceva, a Jewish chief priest, were doing this. But the evil spirit retorted, "I know and recognize and acknowledge Jesus, and I know about Paul, but as for you, who are you?" Then the man, in whom was the evil spirit, leaped on them and subdued all of them and overpowered them, so that they ran out of that house [in terror, stripped] naked and wounded."* (AMPC)

Religion isn't enough to take authority over demons. Simply using the name of Jesus without the assurance of our dominion in Christ will not take control of demonic situations. People can know about God and know about His Holy Spirit, and they can have head knowledge of the truth, but still fail to win the battles against the demonic realm. Having information and walking boldly in authority through the anointing of the Holy Ghost are two entirely different foundations.

It is possible for us to bring deliverance and spiritual help to others through our faith, shielding them in their infancy or youth in Christ. After the new birth, the baby Christians will need spiritual leaders above them to teach them to fight and to protect them until they are able to stand alone. In the Church, leaders are to hold the same job as a parent. They are to help the new believers learn and grow, and they are to teach their people to fight the fight of faith.

However, just as it is possible to train into righteousness, responsibility, and proper sound doctrine, it is also possible to train children into improper patterns of thinking and behaving. In the 21st century, plenty of people both within and outside of the Church fail to grow up and function as healthy contributing members of society.

People who are never confronted for their poor performance or behavior will inevitability be weaker than those who are properly trained with the word of God. Proverbs 27:17 explains, *"As iron sharpens iron, so one person sharpens another."* To be sharp, one must be sharpened, through loving and constructive communication, reproof, discipline, and correction.

Spiritual leaders/parents of the new converts must train the child in faith and in responsibility, or the child is left vulnerable and exposed to the enemy's attacks. Teaching helplessness and irresponsibility will contribute to church members having a lifelong disability where they will continue needing assistance from others, when their God-given destiny is to rise and rescue others.

Human beings who are not taught to take responsibility for their lives will begin to blame others and act out of emotion and other reactive states of mind. This will flip God's design for us on it's head and permit the enemy to lead people, instead of people leading him. And as humans begin to feel out of control because of the misunderstanding of their purpose, strength, and personal decision making, the enemy will creep in and fully overtake them within their situations dictating the outcomes of their lives.

Some churches fail to teach the full counsel of God's Word and this has severe implications for the Church and for the world. *"For I did not shrink from declaring to you the whole purpose and plan of God"* (Acts 20:27, Amplified). These churches resort to teaching "milk" only, and they remain in elementary teachings about Christ, which we are specifically warned not to do by the early disciples.

"Therefore let us move beyond the elementary teachings about Christ and be taken forward to maturity, not laying again the foundation of repentance from acts that lead to death, and of faith in God, instruction about cleansing rites, the laying on of hands, the resurrection of the dead, and eternal judgment. (Hebrews 6:1-2, NIV).

First Corinthians 3:2-3 tells us that if a leader is only teaching elementary doctrine, then they are not yet spiritual and are still carnal (natural) in their thinking and behaving. This is an insult to the Christian, as a Christian should want to mature, grow, and develop into a high functioning spiritually minded member of the Church of Jesus Christ.

"I fed you with milk, not solid food, for you were not yet strong enough [to be ready for it]; but even yet you are not strong enough [to be ready for it], For you are still [unspiritual, having the nature] of the flesh [under the control of ordinary impulses]. For as long as [there are] envying and jealousy and wrangling and factions among you, are you not unspiritual and of the flesh, behaving yourselves after a human standard and like mere (unchanged) men?" (AMPC)

According to Hebrews, laying on of hands and raising people from the dead is elementary; as is fleeing from immorality and sin. Why then do so many Christian leaders proclaim Christ and yet not do His works? Why is there a disconnect between their actions and their words? Consider this passage from Titus 1:10, *"For there are many who are insubordinate, empty talkers and deceivers, especially those of the circumcision party.* (ESV)

Religious people are notorious for using their words without demonstration. Those who work within the ministry, but fail to do the work of the ministry are to be rebuked and publicly addressed.

Titus 1:11-15 explains, *"<u>They must be silenced,</u> since they are upsetting whole families by teaching for shameful gain what they ought not to teach. One of the Cretans, a prophet of their own, said, "Cretans are always liars, evil beasts, lazy gluttons." This testimony is true. <u>Therefore rebuke them sharply,</u> that they may be sound in the faith, not devoting themselves to Jewish myths and the commands of people who turn away from the truth"* (Emphasis added ESV).

Contrary to the American modern societies' belief, Scripture instructs us to rebuke and silence church leaders who are teaching the Bible in error. We are called to take a firm stand in the world, addressing both believers and non-believers, to provide them with the opportunity to hear and embrace the truth.

Whether you are a leader or you are a new believer being deceived and walking in incorrect doctrine is dangerous. The devil will use ignorance and deception to lead anyone he can away from the truth, and once he gets people away from God's truth, then they have no protection.

"Then the devil took him to the holy city and had him stand on the highest point of the temple. "If you are the Son of God," he said, "throw yourself down. For it is written:" 'He will command his angels concerning you, and they will lift you up in their hands, so that you will not strike your foot against a stone' "(Matthew 4:5, NIV)

A refusal to walk in God's plan for our lives is the only time we can be destroyed by the enemy. If Satan would have been successful in tempting Jesus to step outside of God's plan, he could have harmed Jesus. Angelic and supernatural help is only available if we stay in service and obedience to God, not if we step or walk continuously outside of it.

Psalm 91:11 explains, *"For He will command His angels in regard to you, To protect and defend and guard you in all your ways [of obedience and service]."* (AMPC)

As we are walking where God has instructed us to walk and doing the things we are called to do, we don't have to be afraid or careful because we cannot be touched by the enemy's forces. God keeps us safe and guards us in all our ways. We have nothing to fear as we dwell in the shadow of the most high. It is only when people stop dwelling in God and they give way to deceptive lying spirits that they can be captured and taken into captivity.

Samson was a man who was born to overcome all of his enemies. The scriptures tell us he was special and set apart from his mother's womb. Yet Samson disobeyed his mothers instructions. He walked outside of the protection of God by disobeying and disregarding the advice of his elder, his mother, who wanted what was best for him in God.

The Jewish people at large experienced this exact scenario throughout the scriptures. Whenever they strayed from God's commands, believing themselves to be untouchable and invincible against the enemy forces surrounding them, they fell into captivity. However, upon recognizing their disobedience and acknowledging their need for the Lord, they would cry out to Him, and He would once again deliver them from their adversaries. *"If my people who are called by my name humble themselves, and pray and seek my face and turn from their wicked ways, then I will hear from heaven and will forgive their sin and heal their land"* (Second Chronicles 7:14, NIV).

Satan wants us to back off the Word of God. He tries to knock us down and hit us hard so we will become afraid or tired and refuse to continue fighting. In a worst-case scenario, a person willingly stops fighting and bows in weakness, even once, and their life can be destroyed. As it was in the case of Samson, the enemy captured him and took his life, even though God forgave him and allowed him to take out his enemy during his time of death.

The Word of God works, and God comes through on our behalf every time. Even when we feel tired during a fight, we must never back off the Word. If we refuse to back up and back down, the enemy will give up and run from us. He cannot withstand the power of God. He will always give in before we do. Psalm 44:4-5 explains, *"You are my King, O God; Command victories and deliverance for Jacob (Israel). Through You we will gore our enemies [like a bull]; Through Your name we will trample down those who rise up against us."* (AMPC)

If we won't quit the fight, Satan may turn up the heat, but if we keep moving forward in faith, he has no further weapon to use against us. In a season when David thought he had lost a battle against his enemies, he encouraged himself in the Lord. He strengthened himself to continue fighting in the battle, even when he was distraught and tired. As David did this, he discovered he had not lost the battle, even when he thought he was losing everything. He walked away better than he was before, with more possessions.

"And David inquired of the Lord, saying, Shall I pursue this troop? Shall I overtake them? The Lord answered him, Pursue, for you shall surely overtake them and without fail recover all" (First Samuel 30:8, NIV).

Leaders and people in high positions are used either for good or for evil, to sway the masses and lead groups into conformity or rebellion. David was a strong leader. He helped God's people win battles and achieve great things. As God promotes leaders, He strengthens them and their families. He protects all who are involved in His pursuits, and a devoted Christian will always end up better off than they were before they took on the battle with the enemy.

Some of the army refused to fight in the battle with David to recover the things stolen from God's people. They refused to encourage themselves in the Lord, and they claimed they were too fatigued, allowing their physical bodies to dictate their actions rather than their spirits. However, the choice not to fight caused them to not receive the spoil that the rest of the troops received. *"But all the evil men and troublemakers among David's followers said, "Because they did not go out with us, we will not share with them the plunder we recovered. However, each man may take his wife and children and go." * (First Samuel 30:22, NIV).

The refusal to continue fighting caused humiliation for these men and their families. Their choice allowed the enemy to degrade them personally, even when the rest of the army was victorious and radiating with their conquest through God's glory. A refusal to fight will be detrimental to those who give up, but it will never stop the Lord and the courageous children of God from winning and conquering the enemy's forces. We choose if we are going to be the men and women with the spoil or without it.

Not everyone within the house of God experiences the same outcomes, despite having been granted equal access and the same measure of faith. A strong and robust faith only comes from *remaining* in close communion with God, as it is our relationship with God that gives us a proper understanding our identity and the purposes to which we are called. Dwelling in the presence of the Lord has many benefits, and one of them is that we gain clarity regarding our worth and dominion, resulting in a proper appraisal of ourselves and others and this cannot be taken away *if we hold steadfast to it.*

12

False Deities: Worshiping God's Creation

The formal definition of *degradation* is the act or process of damaging and ruining something. To degrade is to take away the beauty and the quality of a thing. It is to ruin, corrupt, and steal the glory and the honor. In the process of degradation, something is made worse and weaker until it is ultimately destroyed. This is the sole mission of the demonic. This is their primary agenda. Satan and all devils work to degrade and diminish the life of the person or the group of people under their domination. They want to steal and spoil the purpose of human life.

In the previous chapter we discussed the men who refused to fight with David and the rest of God's army. This decision to coward in fear caused them to be publicly humiliated. Not only did the humiliation affect the men who refused to fight, but it also affected the women and the children who were under their leadership.

After we are born again, Satan tries to destroy our lives on the battlefield because he wants us to give up and be humiliated as were the men at the brook of Besor. These men and their families should have walked away with the win. They should have been in a season of celebration, and carried God's glory and their testimony, but they allowed their personal weakness to stop them from going forward.

When people are weak and in need of rest in their flesh they can rely on the anointing to pull them through. Christians can encourage themselves in the Lord and do the things mortal men cannot do without the assistance of the Spirit of God. This truth reminds us of our personal responsibility. God will work with us, but we must first decide we want to work with Him. Being strong is a choice not a circumstance.

"Proclaim this among the nations: Prepare for war! Rouse the warriors! Let all the fighting men draw near and attack. Beat your plowshares into swords and your pruning hooks into spears. Let the weakling say, "I am strong!" (Joel 3:9-10, NIV).

Leaning into God and His Holy Spirit will carry us through the battles we could otherwise not enter or win. When God said to rest in His shadow He was instructing us to win in the battles of life by leaning into Him. The choice to dwell closely with God will bring forth tangible and visible protection and strength in this life and the next. The two groups of soldiers following David started in the same place, but they didn't end in the same place because of one groups' choice to rely on God and His Spirit.

Some people refuse to fight back. But when they refuse to engage themselves in the battle, their choice allows Satan to defeat them and humiliate them. Choosing not to engage is not a neutral stance; rather, it signifies a decision of surrender and vulnerability. One in which the enemy will take full advantage of your passivity.

Strong leaders fight for those who are under their leadership. They stand with God and they refuse to allow their feelings or their physical bodies to dictate their choices, because they are led by their spirit. Initially, choices and lifestyles associated with sin may seem to present no immediate consequences. I am sure the men who didn't agree to fight with David were unaware of the negative repercussions to shortly follow their poor choice, because if they knew they had the assured victory they would have continued fighting.

"David and his men reached Ziklag on the third day. Now the Amalekites had raided the Negev and Ziklag. They had attacked Ziklag and burned it, and had taken captive the women and everyone else in it, both young and old. They killed none of them, but carried them off as they went on their way. When David and his men reached Ziklag, they found it destroyed by fire and their wives and sons and daughters taken captive. So David and his men wept aloud until they had no strength left to weep. David's two wives had been captured—Ahinoam of Jezreel and Abigail, the widow of Nabal of Carmel. David was greatly distressed because the men were talking of stoning him; each one was bitter in spirit because of his sons and daughters. But David found strength in the Lord his God" (First Samuel 30:1-6, NIV).

The men who refused to fight were cowards. They accepted defeat in the battle before the battle was complete. They were deceived by their senses; what they could see. So they did what they felt, and they refused to fight back. These men assumed they had already lost their wives and their children, even though this was not the case. Their surrender and inability to press into their fight was the precursor to their ultimate loss. God didn't want them to lose their honor, and dignity. He wanted them to rejoice in the victory and recover all, but because they refused to fight they lost what was theirs.

The first time someone cheats on their spouse or takes the first drink, it often doesn't lead to extreme noticeable consequences. But once the sin takes root in the heart, it will grow, eventually overtaking the person's beauty and their entire life. The spiritual realm operates under seed time and harvest, and every seed we plant or don't plant influences our lives. Good seeds produce good fruit, and bad seeds bring forth bad fruit.

Roots underneath the ground cannot be seen with the human eye. Plants begin growing under the ground and grow upward into a place where we can see, but the roots begin far before we see the fruit. Likewise, when sin or disobedience to God takes root, it begins in the deep places of the earth. It begins where man or woman can't see it fully, because it is a spiritual thing. If it continues to grow and isn't plucked out, it will be harvested and manifest what was planted.

Planting just one evil seed can lead to poisonous plants overtaking a beautiful garden. Satan wants us to believe our choices don't reap consequences as God promised us. But we can be assured both good and evil seeds will develop, and we will harvest whatever we plant if it isn't pulled out of the ground of our hearts. Winning one battle doesn't guarantee we will win another if we don't continue in the anointing and in the faith God has for us. The only way to continue to win is through continual obedience to God and His plan for our lives.

As we consistently nurture God's word in our hearts and seek His guidance for cultivation, we will be spiritually watered, nourished, and safeguarded. We cannot live off of yesterday's bread/manna. As we pray we must pray as God directed us to pray saying: "give us this day our daily bread."

Satan is a defeated foe. He is the top soldier in his military, and he has already been overcome by our commander in chief. God shows us the weakness of Satan. All the world will wonder how he even did the work he did.

Isaiah 14:16-17 says,"Those who see you will gaze at you, They will consider you, saying, 'Is this the man who made the earth tremble, Who shook kingdoms, Who made the world like a wilderness And overthrew its cities, Who did not permit his prisoners to return home?'" (AMPC)

God has given us the weapons we need. We have a better covenant and more power and authority over the enemy than David and his men had under the old covenant. God has prepared us with His Word and His Spirit to win the battles of life. The modern Church will take down giants and overcome the enemy forces by simply staying close to the Lord. We will recover all the enemy has taken from us, and more. Through faith, courage, and perseverance, we will continue to win in any fight. The question is will you fight with us?

We aren't battling Satan because he is more powerful than God or because he has a chance to win in the final battle against God. We are combating Satan because God is giving us more time to work to reach out to more men and women who need to hear the good news of Jesus Christ because they are in the captivity of Satan. Satan knows we already have won the fight. He knows we have the victory over him, and he runs from us, deliberately picking on the people who don't know who they are or what they could use against him.

Our job is to tell people the good news. We are to set the captives free through the Word of God and the demonstration of His Word. Once the truth is heard, believed, and acted on, then people can receive it and be free once and for all. And that is precisely why Satan tries to stop us from speaking up and standing out. Satan doesn't want us openly proclaiming the truth for others to hear and see. He doesn't want us to demonstrate the power of God and publicly shame and humiliate him.

Sin has personal effects, societal effects, and effects on the earth. When people are committing crimes, they need to be punished and stopped from continuing their transgressions. Should a person who is harming others continue to live unpunished for their crimes? Of course not. A good and righteous judge and judicial system would see the crime and punish the criminal on behalf of the victims and the world at large. God, as the ultimate judge of love and mercy, won't permit evil to continue forever.

"The land and the earth also are defiled by their inhabitants, because they have transgressed the laws, disregarded the statutes, and broken the everlasting covenant. Therefore a curse devours the land and the earth, and they who dwell in it suffer the punishment of their guilt. Therefore the inhabitants of the land and the earth are scorched and parched [under the curse of God's wrath], and few people are left" (Isaiah 24:5-6, Amplified).

God's love, mercy, and righteous judgment are the reasons He will judge the earth. But God is waiting today to give the people of the world more time to repent and be saved. Our actions and our words tell a story. They demonstrate and makes clear the distinction between good and evil, salvation and captivity. *Since all these things are to be destroyed in this way, what kind of people ought you to be [in the meantime] in holy behavior [that is, in a pattern of daily life that sets you apart as a believer] and in godliness [displaying profound reverence toward our awesome God]* (Second Peter 3:11, Amplified).

If you have never given your life to Jesus Christ, you can pray the sinner's prayer in the back of this book. By repenting of your sin, you can know you are in right standing with God and going to heaven. Our allegiance to and union with Christ Jesus permits us to win the battles of life and do the works of God through the Holy Spirit. Without Jesus, we all would be beaten up by the enemy like the sons of Sceva the priests who tried to dominate devils without the anointing. Without Christ, we are the men with no strength to take on and win in the battle.

Oftentimes people who are tired or asleep in the Spirit make alliances in battles and don't realize they have made a spiritual alliance with the enemy. Proverbs 18:13 says, "*He who answers before he hears [the facts]— It is folly and shame to him.*" What we hear and what we accept matters because it can bring shame if we hear and respond to a message sent from the enemy.

Some people today attach themselves to doctrines of devils even as members of their local religious communities. They bow to the spirits of the antichrist because they are deceived into following a false doctrine. In the last days men will give way to these doctrines more so than ever. The Bible prophecies with assurance that the evil spirits will cause many to go astray and abandon their faith, leaving the God who loves them and died to save their souls from an eternal hell.

Paul describes such a time: "*For the time will come when people will not tolerate sound doctrine and accurate instruction [that challenges them with God's truth]; but wanting to have their ears tickled [with something pleasing], they will accumulate for themselves [many] teachers [one after another, chosen] to satisfy their own desires and to support the errors they hold, and will* turn their ears away from the truth and will wander off into myths and man-made fictions [and will accept the unacceptable]" (Second Timothy 4:3-4, Amplified).

Paul was warning us of those teachers and religious leaders who would not confront, address, and rebuke sinful lifestyles and choices. He was telling us to beware of the leaders who attest to be following God and yet they lull people to sleep with lies and deception. Once drowsy or asleep, the enemy creeps in and attacks. He overtakes them and destroys their life stealing everything that they have, because their leaders rocked them to sleep after burping them and giving them milk.

God cares about the doctrines we align ourselves with, because our choice shows either an alliance with Him or one with the enemy. God cares if we engage or disengage in a battle, and He wants us to use our faith to win against the forces of evil. The myths and the man-made fictions of the world will lead many astray, as will the exhaustion and the battles of life without the anointing. The Church will thrive and prosper in this last-day move of God, but regular men, without proper doctrine and a close relationship with Christ, will fail because of the fight.

Isaiah 40:31 explains, "*But those who wait for the Lord [who expect, look for, and hope in Him] will gain new strength and renew their power; They will lift up their wings [and rise up close to God] like eagles [rising toward the sun]; They will run and not become weary, they will walk and not grow tired.*" (AMPC)

David sinned against God with Basheba because he stopped engaging in the war. Second Samuel 11:2 says, "*In the spring, at the time when kings go off to war, David sent Joab out with the king's men and the whole Israelite army. They destroyed the Ammonites and besieged Rabbah. But David remained in Jerusalem.*" (AMPC) Let us never stop fighting the fight of faith. Let us never fall asleep and disengage from our battles. As we continue to fight and press into God, we will be renewed, refreshed, and prepared ahead of time for anything the devil has planned to take us out.

Satan has no legal right to dominate and control the believer's life unless we allow him to through our disengagement in battle, or through an enemy alliance. The churches, people, doctrines, and spirits we align ourselves with in every battle determine the outcomes of our lives, and we must be alert and full of meat in the realm of the spirit. Throughout history men and women have partnered with false gods/demon spirits because they were ignorant or indifferent about the consequences of these decisions.

Some cultures have male gods and some have female goddesses, while others have both. Female deities, mentioned in the Bible, such as Asherah and Artemis of Ephesus, have caused many women to ally with the enemy forces. These goddesses promised women fertility, protection in childbirth, and other alluring things. While men traditionally died in battle, women were known to be at risk for death in childbirth, and this fear of death caused women to align themselves with goddesses they believed would shield them.

These gods and goddesses were the center point of the cultures Paul and Timothy were dealing with when Paul instructed Timothy, saying, *"the women should be silent in the churches, for they are not authorized to speak, but are to take a subordinate place, as the Law says."* When Timothy was entrusted with the church as a leader, he was being warned by his elder to stay away from the worship of females and goddesses proclaiming to be superior to the men around them. When these demons rose up and tried to exalt themselves, Paul told Timothy to silence them.

Pastors in the church today need to heed the voice of Paul in this area so they are not asleep in the time of war. We have a mission to silence the demon gods behind the feminist woman or man because if these voices are tolerated, instead of dominated, they will grow in power, creating the Jezebel-/Ahab alliance. Jezebel and Ahab demon rulers, permitted to be in charge, will wreak havoc on God's people and go after the prophets of God seeking their lives. If the devil is permitted to win a battle, he will gain ground and continue to take more.

The decision to not speak God's Word into the atmosphere and into the circumstances of our lives or the lives of others permits the enemy to fill the space with his soldiers. Our silence is often noted as a forfeited or unclaimed territory. In places where Christians do not take their proper place and assert their leadership as a ruler the devil will gladly fill in the space and become ruler of that justification.

The Church must never allow any territory to remain unoccupied, thereby enabling the adversaries of God to exert influence and authority in the world. If Satan has established a stronghold or attempted to dominate a particular area, it is imperative that we assert our authority to expel him from that domain once we become aware of his domination of a person, place, or thing.

There is zero reason to allow demons to function, because we have been given the power and the authority to overcome them. Why would we allow the devils to roam and rule when we can command them to stop and be silent, especially when we know the trajectory they want to take if they aren't commanded to be still. The plans of the devil and his army are all evil. If they are left unchallenged they will destroy people, places, and things.

This earth is the Lords. People are the Lord's. Let us then remove the devils working to harm God's people and His earth. Let us set up Christian camps that heal, restore, and lead people to the truth and authentic freedom. As people come to the camps of God's people they should be refreshed, renewed, and restored from their stay. That is the mission of the Church!

When one of God's prophets speaks, the atmosphere and the lives of the people listening to them will inevitably change as the message is received. Many prophets today, who have been given their positions by God in front of the masses, are being persecuted for speaking out against evil, proclaiming the true message of God. The enemy hates the truth of the messages being sent to the people. He wants to stop the seed of the Word from going forth and changing people's lives for the better, because he wants to keep them in his captivity under his rule.

Prophetic gifts, such as music, acting, or writing, can move people into places of action. Prophets of God and prophets of the devil both use their gift as spiritual warfare, moving the people listening to their prophetic instructions from the god behind the message. This truth should encourage us and cause us to do more, write more, speak more, and act more in the name of Jesus. If we are prohibited from preaching and teaching in the name of Jesus no more, we should smile and know we are making a difference in our world.

So they sent for them, and commanded them not to speak [as His representatives] or teach at all in the name of Jesus [using Him as their authority] (Acts 4:18, Amplified).

Persecutions and accusations from man will never stop the Church. Persecution only strengthens us in our mission. As we continue to use our voice and speak for God, we **proactively** attack Satan. We demonstrate to the world that we are in control and that he is grasping for straws, **trying** to win against us. As we are persecuted and accused, we know it is because we have already won the war and Satan is steadily losing ground.

Women who operate in the anointing are going to be told to shut up and sit down by antichrist spirits, because when they refuse to stop speaking and proclaiming the word of God, they are changing the atmosphere of their society and their culture. Satan hates men and women alike who don't shut up and stop teaching and preaching in authority through Christ. *They will put you out of the synagogues and make you outcasts. And a time is coming when whoever kills you will think that he is offering service to God* (John 16:2, NIV).

Deceived men and women, demanding the subservient and silent nature of women, will throw women out of places of worship, believing they are doing God a service. They will use their mouths to slander, abuse and belittle God's daughters. They will be agents of Satan, acting out as rebellious children in God's house.

"And he said to me, "Son of man, go to the house of Israel and speak with my words to them. For you are not sent to a people of foreign speech and a hard language, but to the house of Israel— not to many peoples of foreign speech and a hard language, whose words you cannot understand. Surely, if I sent you to such, they would listen to you. But the house of Israel will not be willing to listen to you, for they are not willing to listen to me: because all the house of Israel have a hard forehead and a stubborn heart.

Behold, I have made your face as hard as their faces, and your forehead as hard as their foreheads. Like emery harder than flint have I made your forehead. Fear them not, nor be dismayed at their looks, for they are a rebellious house." Moreover, he said to me, "Son of man, all my words that I shall speak to you receive in your heart, and hear with your ears. And go to the exiles, to your people, and speak to them and say to them, 'Thus says the Lord God,' whether they hear or refuse to hear" (Ezekiel 3:4-11, ESV).

God sends His prophets to warn and correct those in His house. He gives rebellious children- those in the Church; not outside of it- a chance to hear the truth and repent for their poor behavior and unholy conduct. And when God sends the prophet the people will either accept and honor the prophet's message or they will turn on the prophet and attempt to kill him. But regardless of the circumstances, God commands His people to persist in speaking the truth and fulfilling the work to which He has called them.

"Whether it is right in the sight of God to listen to you and obey you rather than God, you must judge [for yourselves]; for we, on our part, cannot stop telling [people] about what we have seen and heard" (Acts 4:19-20, Amplified).

The worship of man or woman is disgusting to God. Whether it is through the worshiping and approval of people, or through the worship of the image of man in the form of male or female gods, the worship of the image of a man or a woman is unholy. Fearing man and being overly consumed with the love and the acceptance of human beings entraps humanity. Proverbs 29:25 says, "*The fear of man brings a snare, But whoever trusts in and puts his confidence in the Lord will be exalted and safe.*" (NIV)

In many cultures, men have been exalted so much, the gods are represented by males. Zeus, for instance was a male god who looked like a man. Gods and goddesses resembling humanity is human pride fully manifested. In cultures involved with male worship, women are treated worse than animals and are used as objects for the pleasure and consumption of men alone. Jesus noted the importance of women. He showed the world that they were more important than animals.

"But the Lord replied to him, "You hypocrites (play-actors, pretenders)! Does not each one of you on the Sabbath untie his ox or his donkey from the stall and lead it away to water it? And this woman, a daughter (descendant) of Abraham whom Satan has bound for eighteen long years, should she not have been released from this bond on the Sabbath day?" (Luke 13:15-16, Amplified)

Worshipping the male anatomy, men have abused women and children. It has also destroyed entire communities and countries. The demons of male domination were behind the removal of Queen Vashti. It was through intoxication with the demonic, that these men felt justified and lawful to banish and persecute an innocent woman. The Pharisees were also fooled into feeling justified leaving a woman suffering because they deemed her unworthy of Godly love. In Luke 11:42-54 Jesus says:

"But woe to you, Pharisees! For you tithe mint and rue and every [little] herb, but disregard and neglect justice and the love of God. These you ought to have done without leaving the others undone. Woe to you, Pharisees! For you love the best seats in the synagogues and [you love] to be greeted and bowed down to in the [public] marketplaces.

Woe to you! For you are like graves which are not marked or seen, and men walk over them without being aware of it [and are ceremonially defiled]. One of the experts in the [Mosaic] Law answered Him, Teacher, in saying this, You reproach and outrage and affront even us!

But He said, Woe to you, the lawyers, also! For you load men with oppressive burdens hard to bear, and you do not personally [even gently] touch the burdens with one of your fingers. Woe to you! For you are rebuilding and repairing the tombs of the prophets, whom your fathers killed (destroyed). So you bear witness and give your full approval and consent to the deeds of your fathers; for they actually killed them, and you rebuild and repair monuments to them.

For this reason also the wisdom of God said, I will send them prophets and apostles, [some] of whom they will put to death and persecute, So that the blood of all the prophets shed from the foundation of the world may be charged against and required of this age and generation, From the blood of Abel to the blood of Zechariah, who was slain between the altar and the sanctuary.

Yes, I tell you, it shall be charged against and required of this age and generation. Woe to you, lawyers (experts in the Mosaic Law)! For you have taken away the key to knowledge; you did not go in yourselves, and you hindered and prevented those who were entering. As He left there, the scribes and the Pharisees [followed Him closely, and they] began to be enraged with and set themselves violently against Him and to draw Him out and provoke Him to speak of many things, Secretly watching and plotting and lying in wait for Him, to seize upon something He might say [that they might accuse Him]." (AMPC)

Satan can't force a prophet of God to bow down to him and be quiet, so he tries to intimate and persecute them day and night. He sends leaders and other rulers to try to stop them from their mission. Unfortunately, many of the prophets of old and the prophets of today, male and female, have found their strongest hatred and persecution from within the "synagogues" and modern-day places of worship. Satan tries to stone and murder the prophets with religion and law not secularism.

It happened that as we were on our way to the place of prayer, we were met by a slave-girl who had a spirit of divination [that is, a demonic spirit claiming to foretell the future and discover hidden knowledge], and she brought her owners a good profit by fortune-telling. She followed after Paul and us and kept screaming and shouting, "These men are servants of the Most High God! They are proclaiming to you the way of salvation!"

She continued doing this for several days. Then Paul, being greatly annoyed and worn out, turned and said to the spirit [inside her], "I command you in the name of Jesus Christ [as His representative] to come out of her!" And it came out at that very moment. But when her owners saw that their hope of profit was gone, they seized Paul and Silas and dragged them before the authorities in the market place [where trials were held],

and when they had brought them before the chief magistrates, they said, "These men, who are Jews, are throwing our city into confusion and causing trouble. They are publicly teaching customs which are unlawful for us, as Romans, to accept or observe." The crowd also joined in the attack against them, and the chief magistrates tore their robes off them and ordered that Paul and Silas be beaten with rods (Acts 16:16-22, Amplified).

The demon spirit was unable to directly affect Paul due to the presence of the Holy Spirit within him. Its only means of influence was through another individual in the external realm. Demons understand that they cannot invade or exert control over believers, as they lack the authority to do so. Consequently, their next course of action is to create annoyance and agitation by possessing those around us who have not surrendered their life to Christ.

God has bestowed upon us the power and authority to silence all adversities. We possess the dominion to banish these spirits from our midst whenever they manifest. Once we have removed the person with the spirit or the spirit itself from our lives, the unclean spirits will try again to seek to influence others, both in positions of leadership and among the general populace, aiming to annoy us or persecute us for our alliance with Christ.

However, should they attempt to imprison us or accuse us of transgressing their laws, God will steadfastly support and protect us. He will ensure our freedom and dominion and He will continue to empower us to fulfill our call. *"But about midnight when Paul and Silas were praying and singing hymns of praise to God, and the prisoners were listening to them; suddenly there was a great earthquake, so [powerful] that the very foundations of the prison were shaken and at once all the doors were opened and everyone's chains were unfastened"* (Acts 16:25-26, Amplified).

Let us raise our voices in praise to the Lord and boldly proclaim the truth from the rooftops. No person, deity, or demonic spirit can prevail against our message. We are empowered by a superior force, operating under divine authority. Our God reigns supreme over all, and He has entrusted us with significant responsibility; the opportunity to rule.

13

Loosed - The Siege - Untying the Knot of Satan

Humanity without Christ, lives as captives under Satan's domination. Satan understands the power he holds over a spiritually dead person. The deaf, the blind, and the dumb can't hear, see, or think because they are spiritually dead. A dead person has no ability to properly function or defend themselves. Demon spirits thrive on the flesh of the dead. They feast on those without spiritual vision, hearing, or thought because they are easy victims.

When people are dead spiritually, they increasingly decay by the day, and they don't have any hope outside of revival- the process of being brought back to life. The decaying and rotting flesh draws beasts and nasty creatures. Demon spirits come when they smell and locate someone who is dead.

A vulture is a bird of prey, and it scavenges on dead things. Vultures by their very nature are looking for someone or something to devour, and when they are looking for their prey, they want to find a place to feast and not be challenged. Things that are alive, moving, and willing to fight back aren't bothered by the birds, because the birds are intimated by them.

Demons prey on the dead, or lethargic humans in the Spirit. Spiritually dead humans are easy slaughters for the demonic, as are those who lie motionless. Humans who lie in bed for months at a time will develop lesions and other complications. Bed rot is a condition where motionless people decay, even when they are still alive. The rotting flesh of the person dead or motionless draws the crowd of evil. When the demons come, they find the person is indeed dead or helpless and therefore easy to devour and conquer.

On the contrary, when demons find humans who are spiritually alive, they generally stay away from them because they know they aren't a match for the person who is alive. To be a Christian is to be living with the jurisdiction and convictions of heaven. Through the movement and the thriving nature of the born-again, alive Christian, demons know this individual is not an easy target.

Vultures tear at the flesh of their victims. They pull the victim apart piece by piece and eventually reach the bones, and shortly there will be nothing left. In the same way, demons will begin by oppressing and surrounding the weak. They circle and select whom they will devour, and once they have their victim, they pull them apart, little by little until there is no trace of them left.

Demons know they are inferior to the born-again people of the world. They know God has designated and declared them to be under the foot of a man or woman of God. This truth causes demons to flee from anyone who knows their rightful position in Christ and moves in faith towards their destination. Demons generally want to get away from the Christian moving in faith, because they know they are alive and capable of harming or redirecting them. In a match against a Christian, demons are the prey, not the predator.

While we are alive on the earth, all of us are on a spiritual battlefield. When we are born, we are born into a battle that has been raging for generations. God has given us the His son Jesus Christ, the Holy Spirit, and access to Him in heaven— *the keys to every part of the arsenal.* — God has given us an assured victory over our enemy when we are engaged and moving in our faith on the battlefield. This victory positions us where demons don't want to come near us because they know they are going to be taken out.

"From the days of John the Baptist until now the kingdom of heaven suffers violent assault, and violent men seize it by force [as a precious prize]" (Matthew 11:12, Amplified).

The devil's kingdom is under siege. The Church is taking ground from them, reclaiming people, places, and things, and pushing them into the exact place he doesn't want to be. Our solidified forces are backing Satan and all the demonic armies right into position to be completely taken out in the final battle once and for all.

"I saw heaven standing open and there before me was a white horse, whose rider is called Faithful and True. With justice he judges and wages war. His eyes are like blazing fire, and on his head are many crowns. He has a name written on him that no one knows but he himself. He is dressed in a robe dipped in blood, and his name is the Word of God.

The armies of heaven were following him, riding on white horses and dressed in fine linen, white and clean. Coming out of his mouth is a sharp sword with which to strike down the nations. "He will rule them with an iron scepter." He treads the winepress of the fury of the wrath of God Almighty. On his robe and on his thigh he has this name written: king of kings and lord of lords" (Revelation 19:11-16, NIV).

Being alive and active is what keeps the vultures back. Staying on fire with the Holy Spirit permits us to advance, even when we feel tired in the flesh. In the battle on the mission field, with the Holy Spirit, we will never need to retreat. When we are weak, He is strong on our behalf. If we want to quit, we don't have to because we will be renewed and refreshed supernaturally, because we dwell with God in the Spirit realm.

In one man there lived thousands of demons. Luke 8:30-31 teaches, *"Then Jesus asked him, "What is your name?" And he answered, "Legion"; because many demons had entered him. They continually begged Him not to command them to go into the abyss."*

But Jesus Christ was a threat to this demon army of thousands because they knew they were no match in a battle against Him. In the Roman army, during the earthly ministry of Christ, a legion was typically between 3,000 and 6,000 soldiers, and Jesus Christ effortlessly made 3,000-6,000 demons to tremble.

Even against the most vile and vicious demons who are willing to engage us in a battle, we have the victory. If we are in a battle against a thousand demons, we still can win when we are yoked with Christ. Whether it is a person inspired by a demon or the demons themselves, Joshua 23:10 explains, *"For the Lord has driven out great and mighty nations from before you; and as for you, no man has been able to stand [in opposition] before you to this day. One of your men puts to flight a thousand, for the Lord your God is He who is fighting for you, just as He promised you."* (AMPC)

Demons who attempt to position themselves against the children of God hope they don't know who they are in Christ. Their strategy in a war with a Christian is to trick them to retreat, because when the Christian stands firm, they know they will never win. Some high-ranking demon spirits will attempt to taunt us, but they do their work to cause fear and intimation leading to a retreat. These spirits, like the ones within Goliath, work through threats.

I have only seen a few unclean spirits. Two of the demon spirits who revealed themselves to me were taunting spirits. The first mocked God and said to me in a dream: *"Do you think you can cast me out in the name of Jesus? Ha ha ha ha ha."* The second demon had a similar attitude and showed me a congregation of saints singing and praising God in a room. When the demon showed me the people, it taunted me, asserting that the Church was weak and unable to help me, and it used a scripture to "verify" what it was saying.

The scripture the unclean spirit used to try to make me afraid of it was Deuteronomy 32:30: *"One of your men puts to flight a thousand, for the LORD your God is He who is fighting for you, just as He promised you."* But when the spirit spoke this verse to me, it was insinuating no one within the church could come against it and cause it to flee as God said. Demons' primary weapon against the Christian is fear and retreat, and they use this weapon hoping to cause a believer to surrender. Through lying and intimating, demons deceive whoever allows them to cause panic within them and stop the battle against them.

Without a full understanding of who we are Christ; Christians will respond to these unclean spirits in a manner like the Israelite army before David arrived on the battlefield. When a Christian isn't full of the Holy Spirit and absolutely assured of their victory, the enemy will press up against them and try to take whatever they can take from the child of God. Devils don't play nice or fair. They fight dirty and steal anything they are given access to.

First Samuel 17:23-24 teaches, *"As he was talking with them, Goliath, the Philistine champion from Gath, stepped out from his lines and shouted his usual defiance, and David heard it. Whenever the Israelites saw the man, they all fled from him in great fear."* (NIV)

David was used to fighting. He was accustomed to destroying the lions and the bears of the wilderness. David knew the loud, aggressive, taunting spirit would go down in a fight if he confronted him in God's power and authority. David's identity as a child of God was secure, and he was sure he was the predator, not the prey. He was a threat to evil forces, not a victim. David's assurance in his identity with God was the key to the victory in battle. It was the key that opened the doors for success in his life.

"But David said to Saul, "Your servant has been keeping his father's sheep. When a lion or a bear came and carried off a sheep from the flock, I went after it, struck it and rescued the sheep from its mouth. When it turned on me, I seized it by its hair, struck it and killed it. Your servant has killed both the lion and the bear; this uncircumcised Philistine will be like one of them, because he has defied the armies of the living God" (First Samuel 17:34-36, NIV).

Goliath teased David: *""Come here," he said, "and I'll give your flesh to the birds and the wild animals!"* (First Samuel 17:44, NIV). Goliath was signaling to demon spirits and other unclean men within his army, in-sinuating he was going to give David over to them if David would bow down in fear before him. The truth is, if David had bowed down to Goliath, he would have been preyed upon by the hosts of demons and unclean men waiting to pounce on their prey, but since he refused to coward in fear, he took authority over the enemy.

One time when my family and I were on a vacation in the Smokey Mountains of Tennessee, we encountered a bear in the woods. There was no one around but my husband, my oldest son, my daughter, and me in those backwoods. When the bear saw us and we saw it, we didn't run or allow our kids to run either. We backed away from the animal slowly, staring it in the eyes, and we never turned our back to it run-ning away.

In nature, when humans encounter a wild animal, such as a bear, and the animal perceives that humans are afraid and weak, it will of-ten pounce and attack the human being. Yet if a person remains firm and strong and stands their ground, challenging the animal, it will de-termine it is the weakest in the battle and retreat. Demonic beings are the same way. They know who is going to confront them and look at them in faith, and who is going to run and hide in fear.

"David ran and stood over him. He took hold of the Philistine's sword and drew it from the sheath. After he killed him, he cut off his head with the sword. When the Philistines saw that their hero was dead, they turned and ran. Then the men of Israel and Judah surged forward with a shout and pursued the Philistines to the entrance of Gath and to the gates of Ekron. Their dead were strewn along the Shaaraim road to Gath and Ekron" (First Samuel 17:51-52, NIV).

Christian leaders have an important job of keeping the snakes, vul-tures, bears, lions, and other beasts in the Spirit back from the flock of the Lord. The position of a shepherd is an honor, but it is also a re-sponsibility. Shepherds must lead the younger sheep to victory. They must teach people to stand boldly in their position against their en-emy. We taught our children that day in the woods to not run from the bear, but if we had allowed them to run away in fear, the situation may have turned out differently.

In the lives of David, Esther, Deborah, Ezra, and many other heroic leaders, the bold strength and faith infused in them from God inspired others to move forward in faith. Leaders, the commanders in God's army have a mission to teach and preach faith to the people so the people can rise, respond, and move in accordance with the commands of God. The movement of the armies of the Lord will keep the demon forces back, and it will stop the enemy from pushing us around.

All of us, regardless of our current rank and position should be sincere, hardworking, and reliable. In our military position, there are different occupations and positions, and each of us has been strategically assigned to our places by the Lord. New converts and young people in their faith benefit from the strong leadership of the elders. The elders likewise can benefit from the hard work and diligence of new converts when each of us knows our God–given place and works conscientiously where we have been positioned.

Let everything you do be done in love (true love to God and man as inspired by God's love for us). You know that the household of Stephanas were the first converts in Achaia, and they have devoted themselves to the service of the Lord's people. I urge you, brothers and sisters, to submit to such people and to everyone who joins in the work and labors at it. I was glad when Stephanas, Fortunatus and Achaicus arrived, because they have supplied what was lacking from you. For they refreshed my spirit and yours also. Such men deserve recognition (First Corinthians 16:14-18).

If we evaluate ourselves properly, we will not need to be judged by God or by man. Having an honest and humble opinion of ourselves and of our position in the house of God will keep us from error and problems. The family of God is the apple of God's eye. God watches over His House and His children, and He corrects those who refuse to correct themselves when they hurt another in the family. Our behavior towards people in the house is even more important than those outside of it.

First Corinthians 11:29-31 explains, *"For anyone who eats and drinks [without solemn reverence and heartfelt gratitude for the sacrifice of Christ], eats and drinks a judgment on himself if he does not recognize the body [of Christ]. That [careless and unworthy participation] is the reason why many among you are weak and sick, and a number sleep [in death]. But if we evaluated and judged ourselves honestly [recognizing our shortcomings and correcting our behavior], we would not be judged."* (AMPC)

God places people over our head to lead us and help us, and as we mature in Him, He will place us over others to lead and help them. Whether we lead one person or one million people, God watches to see if we are hardworking, kind, loving, edifying, and honest. There is never a day or a decision we make that escapes the Lord. Every decision, whether pure or impure, is seen and remembered. First Corinthians 16:16 explains, *"I urge you to pay all deference to such leaders and to enlist under them and be subject to them, as well as to everyone who joins and cooperates [with you] and labors earnestly."* (AMPC)

Advancing God's mission as a family and a team is our goal as the Church. We are not in competition with each other, and we should never work against our brothers and sisters in faith. Our army doesn't need to be separated by the characteristics of male, female, race, nationality, or background. When we fight, we need to see the emblem on the arms of the soldier's coat alone. If we see a soldier in God's army, regardless of their physical appearances, we greet them with respect and love, honor and grace, knowing we are on the same team and on the same mission.

Rahab was supposed to be destroyed with the people of her land. She was to be wiped out because her people didn't serve and honor God. Rahab was a Canaanite, and she was associated with a group of people who were against God's kingdom. However, Rahab protected the two spies sent by Joshua, and she became an ancestor of Jesus because she chose to make an alliance with God's army. Rahab's "coat" she placed outside of her house signaled to the soldiers that she was an ally, not an enemy.

The background of a person, the gender, race, or societal group we were a part of prior to our salvation doesn't determine our fate in the battle between good and evil. Our choice to join ourselves to Christ, and to God's house, through faith and love, is the only determining factor of our fate. As we take off the enemy's coat and align ourselves with the armies of heaven, we can know we will be spared in the battles of life. We know we will live and not die, even when the rest of the people around us perish in the war.

Joshua son of Nun sent two men secretly from Shittim as scouts, saying, Go, view the land, especially Jericho. And they went and came to the house of a harlot named Rahab and lodged there. It was told the king of Jericho, Behold, there came men in here tonight of the Israelites to search out the country. And the king of Jericho sent to Rahab, saying, Bring forth the men who have come to you, who entered your house, for they have come to search out the land. But the woman had taken the two men and hidden them. So she said, Yes, two men came to me, but I did not know from where they had come. And at gate closing time, after dark, the men went out. Where they went I do not know. Pursue them quickly, for you will overtake them. But she had brought them up to the roof and hidden them under the stalks of flax which she had laid in order there. So the men pursued them to the Jordan as far as the fords. As soon as the pursuers had gone, the city's gate was shut. Before the two men had lain down, Rahab came up to them on the roof, And she said to the men, I know that the Lord has given you the land and that your terror is fallen upon us and that all the inhabitants of the land faint because of you.

For we have heard how the Lord dried up the water of the Red Sea for you when you came out of Egypt, and what you did to the two kings of the Amorites who were on the [east] side of the Jordan, Sihon and Og, whom you utterly destroyed. When we heard it, our hearts melted, neither did spirit or courage remain any more in any man because of you, for the Lord your God, He is God in heaven above and on earth beneath. Now then, I pray you, swear to me by the Lord, since I have shown you kindness, that you also will show kindness to my father's house, and give me a sure sign, And save alive my father and mother, my brothers and sisters, and all they have, and deliver us from death. And the men said to her, Our lives for yours! If you do not tell this business of ours, then when the Lord gives us the land we will deal kindly and faithfully with you. (Joshua 2:1-15)

Joshua's and Caleb's alliance with Rahab assured protection for her and her family. As Rahab involved herself in the battle for God, she aided in God's mission against His enemy. Her decisions to align herself with God and His troops rewarded her with life. Out of a respect for the mission of God, these men and women looked at the coat of armor worn by the solider, not the gender, the background, or the race. Rahab was formerly a harlot, a woman not associated with God, but through a decision of faith and a willful alliance, Rahab became one of the great women of the Bible impacting the history of God's people as we know it.

God makes His selections for His family based on the heart of the man/woman. He looks at the intention, the loyalty, and the heart of the person. As God's people, we will honor God by acting like Him. We too will choose to step outside of race, gender, or other social groupings. The family of God is multigenerational and multicultural. It is a family of men, women, and children. Thank God for the family we have in Christ. Let us show honor and respect to every solider who bears God's name. We are either with Him, or we are against Him and the choice is ours.

Matthew 12:30 teaches, *"He who is not with Me [once and for all on My side] is against Me; and he who does not [unequivocally] gather with Me scatters."* (AMPC)

A Message to the People of God

Stay faithful and never bow down to evil. Only those who perse-vere in faith, love, and diligence will win in the battles of life. For those who leave the sheep without a shepherd, who run from the wolves, the lions, and the beasts of the earth, and to those who refuse to take their proper place as a leader in the household of faith, you will be judged more harshly for your injustice against your brothers and sisters. Choose today to take your position against the enemy and not bow down to any enemy, big or small. Do the work of God. Save souls and work with anyone and everyone who cares about God and His kingdom. Don't be foolish. Choose to be wise and discern the truth, that the Lord uses men and women, black and white, rich and poor, Jew or Gentile, to do the work of the kingdom and continue His mis-sions. We are here together to fight this battle against our enemy, Sa-tan. We are positioned purposefully as a unit to retrieve the lost and the captive souls.

"Roam back and forth through the streets of Jerusalem, And look now and take note. And look in her open squares To see if you can find a man [as Abraham sought in Sodom], One who is just, who [has integrity and moral courage and] seeks truth (faithfulness); Then I will pardon Jerusalem—[for the sake of one uncompromisingly righteous person]. "And although they say, 'As the Lord lives,' Certainly they swear falsely."

O Lord, do not Your eyes look for truth? You [have seen their faithless heart and] have stricken them, But they did not weaken; You have consumed them, But they refused to take correction or instruction. They have made their faces harder than rock; They have refused to repent and return to You. Then I said, "[Surely] these are only the poor (uneducated); They are [sinfully] foolish and have no [spiritual] understanding, For they do not know the way of the Lord Or the ordinance of their God [and the requirements of His just and righteous law].

"I will go to the great [men] And speak to them, For they [must] know the way of the Lord, The ordinance of their God." But [I found the reverse to

be true, that] they too had all alike broken the yoke [of God's law] And had burst the bonds [of obedience to Him]. Therefore a lion from the forest will kill them, A wolf of the deserts will destroy them, A leopard is watching their cities. Everyone who goes out of them shall be torn in pieces, Because their transgressions are many, Their desertions of faith are countless.

"Why should I [overlook these offenses and] forgive you? Your children have abandoned (rejected) Me And sworn [their oaths] by those who are not gods. When I had fed them until they were full [and bound them to Me by a promise], They committed [spiritual] adultery, Assembling in troops at the houses of prostitutes (idols). "They were like well-fed, lusty stallions, Each one neighing after his neighbor's wife.

"Shall I not punish them [for these things]?" says the Lord; "Shall I not avenge Myself On a nation such as this?" "Go up through the rows of Jerusalem's vineyards and destroy [them], But do not completely destroy everything. Strip away her branches and the tendrils [of her vines], For they are not the Lord's. "For the house of Israel and the house of Judah Have dealt very treacherously (faithlessly) with Me," declares the Lord.

They have lied about and denied the Lord By saying, "It is not He [who speaks through His prophets]; Misfortune and evil shall not come on us, Nor will we see war or famine. "The prophets are like the wind [their prophecy will not come to pass], And the word [of God] is not in them. In this manner it will be done to them [as they prophesied, not to us]."

Therefore, thus says the LORD God of hosts, "Because you [people] have spoken this word, Behold, I am making My words a fire in your mouth [Jeremiah] And this people wood, and My words will consume them. "Behold, I am bringing a nation against you from far away, O house of Israel," says the LORD. "It is a mighty and enduring nation, It is an ancient nation, A nation whose language you do not know, Whose words you do not comprehend.

"Their quiver is [filled with the dead] like an open grave; They are all mighty men [heroes of their nation]. "They will consume your harvest and [eat up] your bread; They will consume your sons and your daughters; They will consume your flocks and your herds; They will consume your vines and your fig trees. With the sword they will break down and demolish your fortified cities in which you trust. "But even in those days," says the Lord, "I will not totally destroy you.

It will come about when your people say, 'Why has the Lord our God done all these things to us?' then you shall answer them, 'As you have abandoned (rejected) Me,' [says the Lord,] 'and have served strange and foreign gods in your land, so you will serve strangers in a land that is not yours.' "Declare this in the house of Jacob And proclaim it in Judah, saying: 'Now hear this, O foolish people without heart, Who have eyes but do not see, Who have ears but do not hear. 'Do you not fear Me?' says the LORD. 'Do you not tremble [in awe] in My presence? For I have placed the sand as a boundary for the sea, An eternal decree and a perpetual barrier beyond which it cannot pass. Though the waves [of the sea] toss and break, yet they cannot prevail [against the sand ordained to hold them back]; Though the waves and the billows roar, yet they cannot cross over [the barrier]. [Is not such a God to be feared?]

'But this people has a stubborn heart and a rebellious will [that draws them away from Me]; They have turned away and have gone [into idolatry]. 'They do not say in their heart, "Let us now fear and worship the Lord our God [with profound awe and reverence], Who gives rain in its season, Both the autumn and the spring rain, Who keeps for us The appointed weeks of the harvest." 'Your wickedness has turned these [blessings] away, And your sins have withheld good [harvests] from you. 'For wicked men are found among My people, They watch like fowlers who lie in wait; They set a trap, They catch men. 'As a cage is full of birds, So are their houses full of deceit and treachery; Therefore they have become influential and rich.

'They are fat and they are sleek (prosperous), They excel in acts of wickedness; They do not plead the cause, The cause of the orphan, so that they [the wicked] may prosper, And they do not defend the rights of the poor. 'Shall I not punish them [for these things]?' says the Lord. 'Shall I not avenge Myself On such a nation as this?' "An appalling and horrible thing [bringing desolation and destruction] Has come to pass in the land: The prophets prophesy falsely, And the priests rule on their own authority; And My people love [to have] it so! But what will you do when the end comes?" (Jeremiah 5:1-31, Amplified)

14

Blessings & Curses

Psalm 1:1-8 says, *"Blessed [fortunate, prosperous, and favored by God] is the man who does not walk in the counsel of the wicked [following their advice and example], Nor stand in the path of sinners, Nor sit [down to rest] in the seat of scoffers (ridiculers). But his delight is in the law of the Lord, and on His law [His precepts and teachings] he [habitually] meditates day and night. And he will be like a tree firmly planted [and fed] by streams of water, which yields its fruit in its season; Its leaf does not wither; And in whatever he does, he prospers [and comes to maturity]. The wicked [those who live in disobedience to God's law] are not so, But they are like the chaff [worthless and without substance] which the wind blows away. Therefore, the wicked will not stand [unpunished] in the judgment, Nor sinners in the assembly of the righteous. For the Lord knows and fully approves the way of the righteous, But the way of the wicked shall perish."* (AMPC)

God's blessing is available to be manifested in this life and the next, and the blessing is paramount for success. A person who has been pronounced with God's blessing is distinctively different than a person who lives underneath the curse. God's blessing impacts every part of our lives. It shapes who we are, what we do, and what we have.

When you are a child of God, you are a distinct creation; a creation who is not perishing. God's children are alive and thriving when the world around them isn't, and as a result they carry with them something marking and signifying this truth. Once the blessing of the Lord comes onto a person's life, it cannot be taken away by any man, woman, or demonic entity. The blessing is given by God and nothing can stand against it.

The blessing is accessed through salvation and faith in God. There is a reward for obeying and honoring God. All of humanity has been given a choice to remain under the curse or to come into blessing, yet many refuse to receive their inheritance.

Being born again and becoming one with Christ is the only prerequisite to becoming an heir to the blessings, privileges, and rights of a child of God. We read in Galatians 3:13 and 3:29, *"In order that in Christ Jesus the blessing of Abraham might also come to the Gentiles, so that we would all receive [the realization of] the promise of the [Holy] Spirit through faith. And if you belong to Christ [if you are in Him], then you are Abraham's descendants, and [spiritual] heirs according to [God's] promise."* (AMPC)

Foolish men and women set themselves against God, by setting themselves against God's blessed people. These individuals don't respect and recognize God's blessing on His people's lives so they choose to disrespect those whom God has honored and ordained to perform His work on the earth.

Wicked and foolish people attempt to curse or harm those whom the Lord has called and blessed. Trying to put a curse on God's anointed regardless of who you are is sin against God and can bring calamity into a life. Numbers 23:8 says, *"But how can I curse those whom God has not cursed? How can I denounce those whom the Lord has not denounced."* (AMPC)

Some members of the Church fail to acknowledge and appropriately honor others within God's family. If this behavior persists, they will face unnecessary struggles. Attempts to undermine and dishonor others in the household of faith often stem from a misguided sense of superiority; however, such actions are ultimately sinful in the eyes of God. Factors such as gender, race, age, or other external characteristics often contribute to the dishonoring of God's saints. Nevertheless, it is unequivocal that God does not condone these harmful actions, nor does He support such behavior.

In a household setting parents monitor their children and ensure they are interacting with one another in appropriate ways. If a sibling is unkind to another the parents often step in and put a stop to it out of mercy and compassion. God wants to teach His children to love one another. He wants to make sure we are not mistreating anyone in the household of faith.

God informs us as the Church we will face persecution from those outside of the Church. Thus, it is of upmost importance that we never do work for the enemy harming another Christian. It is the plan of the devil to have Christians attacking other Christians. For the Church to properly advance we must work together, build each other up, and operate as a family enlisted against all forces of darkness.

If a church member takes a vicious stance against another brother or sister the Lord will attempt to correct them in love. It is wise then to receive His rebuke and change the behavior, so the Church can live among each other in a healthy way. If a member refuses to respect another it will hinder their walk while potentially wounding someone God wants to honor and bless.

Consider First Peter 3:7 where the Lord tells husbands they can hinder their prayers by treating their wife with disrespect. *"In the same way, you husbands, live with your wives in an understanding way [with great gentleness and tact, and with an intelligent regard for the marriage relationship], as with someone physically weaker, since she is a woman. Show her honor and respect as a fellow heir of the grace of life, so that your prayers will not be hindered or ineffective."* (AMPC)

This principle applies for all aspects of Christian family and interaction. We must be kind and respectful to one another if we are going to rise higher and position ourselves for the outpouring of blessings of God.

Scripture tells us Nabal was a man who, because of his wealth, showed no respect to God's blessed and anointed servant David. Nabal foolishly perceived David as inferior to himself. Nabal believed his money and social standing would protect him, and Nabal didn't consider God. First Samuel 25:10 states, *"Nabal answered David's servants, 'Who is this David? Who is the son of Jesse? Many servants are breaking away from their masters these days. Why should I take my bread and water, and the meat I have slaughtered for my shears, and give it to men coming from who knows where?'"* (AMPC)

Nabal's stance against David was a stance against God, because God was partnering with David. When Nabal failed to recognize God's alliance with David, Nabal disrespected the Lord and the Lord's plan. Nabal attempted to curse David, whom God had blessed, but in the process, Nabal lost his own life. First Samuel 25:38 explains, *"About ten days later, the Lord struck Nabal, and he died."* (AMPC)

Today, as in the days of David, some set themselves up against God's chosen people, and in doing, so they resist God's plans and purposes. Like Nabal, these men and women unknowingly trust in human resources, ignoring the hand of God, and in doing so endanger themselves because they position themselves against God.

Nabal was not the first or the last fool to fall at the hands of God's servant David. Goliath and King Saul were two other men who suffered the same shameful fate by trusting in their own strength and abilities while dealing foolishly with David. All three men made separate decisions to trust in their humanity and their worldly positions of power and authority instead of relying on God's power and authority. Although their authority and positions were different, their hearts and positions towards David's assignment to fulfill God's mission for the earth was the same.

When David was just a boy, he was able to defeat Goliath. Goliath believed that he would defeat David because he was a man of war. Goliath was used to fighting his battles with swords, spears, and other weaponry. Goliath trusted in his weapons and his own body stature. He trusted in false gods.

Goliath's trust in his fighting abilities and in his weaponry emboldened him to mock God and God's people. Goliath was prepared in the natural realm for a fight, but Goliath had never fought in the spirit against a believer, and he was unprepared for spiritual battle. Goliath's physical attributes couldn't protect him. God doesn't care about what we look like on the outside. He cares about who we are on the inside.

First Samuel 17 declares,

"David said to the Philistine, 'You come against me with sword and spear and javelin, but I come against you in the name of the Lord Almighty, the God of the armies of Israel, who you have defiled. This day the Lord will deliver you into my hands, and I'll strike you down and cut off your head. This very day I will give the carcasses of the Philistine army to the birds and the wild animals, and the whole world will know there is a God in Israel. All those gathered here will know that it is not by sword or spear that the Lord saves; for the battle is the Lords, and He will give all of you into our hands.'"

David was blessed from a young age. As a boy, David loved God with his whole heart, so God exalted David early in his life. David was noticeably different from the others around him. He was given a special position within society not because of what he looked like, but because of who He honored and served. God promoted David because David was willing to surrender his entire life to God's plans and pursuits.

David was willing to be a vessel that chased after God and God's interests instead of his own. David's humble and respectful mindset and heart enabled him to be blessed and to partner with God. First Samuel 13:14 says, *"But now your kingdom shall not continue; the Lord has sought out [David] a man after His own heart, and the Lord has commanded him to be prince and ruler over his people, because you have not kept what the Lord commanded you."* (AMPC)

Unlike his adversaries, David didn't trust in his own strength and ability. David's trust was in the Lord's strength and ability. David respected God as the Almighty One, and he gave honor to God. David was humble, and he knew that he needed God to be successful.

Throughout his life, David continuously magnified the Lord's goodness, ability, and power instead of magnifying his own. David's desire to please and honor God caused God to protect, elevate, and assist David.

When David's enemies put their trust in money, armory, or political position, David's trust remained unwavering in the Lord. King Saul was one of David's enemies, and it appeared as if Saul would reign victoriously over David, because he was the king holding political power. Yet, many times when King Saul tried to kill David, the Lord protected David. Even the King could not harm David. First Samuel 23:14 tells us, *"David stayed in the wilderness strongholds and in the hills of the Desert of Ziph. Day after day Saul searched for him, but God did not give David into his hands."* (AMPC)

David's life is a testament of the blessing's ability to make an individual safe and untouchable by enemy forces. David's story also shows the importance of an alliance with God's chosen vessels. Saul's son Jonathan made the wise choice to respect God by respecting David and David's position with God. As a result of this decision, Jonathan was blessed, even when his father became cursed. First Samuel 20:16 explains, *"So Jonathan made a covenant with the house of David, saying, 'May the Lord call David's enemies to account.' And Jonathan had David reaffirm his oath out of love for him, because he loved him as he loved himself."* (AMPC)

Abigail, the wife of David's adversary Nabal also decided to side with the Lord when she recognized and respected David as a servant of the Lord. Abigail's decision was courageous! In faith, Abigail faced a powerful army seeking to kill her entire household. Abigail understood that God would keep her safe and not allow her to suffer harm if she honored and respected David and his position. Even when Abigail's husband, Nabal's, life was ended prematurely, Abigail and her household were not killed.

When Abigail saw David, she quickly got off her donkey and bowed down before David with her face to the ground. She fell at his feet and said: *"Pardon your servant, my lord, and let me speak to you; hear what your servant has to say. Please pay no attention, my lord, to that wicked man Nabal. He is just like his name—his name means fool, and folly goes with him. And as for me, your servant, I did not see the men my lord sent. And now, my lord, as surely as the Lord your God lives and as you live, since the Lord has kept you from bloodshed and from avenging yourself with your own hands, may your enemies and all who are intent on harming my lord be like Nabal. And let this gift, which your servant has brought to my lord, be given to the men who follow you. Please forgive your servant's presumption. The Lord your God will certainly make a lasting dynasty for my lord, because you fight the Lord's battles, and no wrongdoing will be found in you as long as you live. Even though someone is pursuing your life, the life of my lord will be bound securely in the bundle of the living by the Lord your God, but the lives of your enemies he will hurl away as from the pocket of a sling"* (First Samuel 25: 23–31, NIV).

God protects anyone who chooses to take refuge in Him. He exalts and blesses those who honor Him in front of their enemies. The Bible promises that the people who love God and love His name will rejoice and sing for joy because the Lord keeps them safe from trouble. Psalms 5:11 teaches us, *"But let all who take refuge in you be glad; let them ever sing for joy. Spread your protection over them, so that those who love your name may rejoice in you."* (NIV)

Refuge is the condition of being safe or sheltered from pursuit, danger, or trouble. Many powerful men were humbled or brought to nothing in front of David, because he was humble, and he trusted in the refuge of the Lord.

When the devil attempts to inflict pain, suffering, turmoil, or any form of destruction upon the believer, the believer must stand firm, resisting the attack, confidently knowing the Lord will fight on his or her behalf. Often, the devil sends conflict, trouble, or problems into a believer's life, hoping the believer will not resist him and will, instead, accept the attack.

Yet, the devil cannot prevail when a believer chooses to take refuge in the Holy Scriptures and rests in the wings of God. God is our safe place. He is our bomb shelter when we experience serious warfare.

The devil has been allowed to roam the earth for a certain amount of time. God cast the devil and the demons out of heaven thousands of years ago, yet they are still roaming the earth and tormenting people. The devil uses humanity to further perpetrate his evil agenda on the earth.

God allows for the wicked to prosper for an allotted time. God lets evil people continue in their evil to ultimately be harshly punished for their deeds. Proverbs 16:4 teaches, *"The Lord has a reason for everything he does, and he lets evil people live only to be punished."* (NIV)

God cannot be defeated, and He often uses the devil's own stupidity, rebellion, and hatred of Him to further His own plans and pursuits. We see this theme all throughout scripture. For instance, the devil believed he was defeating the Lord when he had humanity crucify Jesus. The devil wrongfully believed by crucifying Jesus, he would be able to stop Jesus, and God would be defeated. He believed he could stop God's word from being fulfilled.

God's wisdom far exceeds the devil's schemes and plans. God ensures what the devil means for evil will be turned around for good. Satan didn't take Jesus' life from Him. Jesus could have called on the armies of heaven to destroy everyone and everything around Him, but He chose to go to the cross. John 10:18 says, *"No one takes it from me, but I lay it down of my own accord. I have authority to lay it down and authority to take it up again. This command I received from my Father."*

Many verses in the Old Testament told of Jesus's coming. The devil knew God's servants prophesied about the destruction of his kingdom on earth. The devil knew God said he would be destroyed by a king born from God's lineage. Throughout the centuries, the devil has attempted to stop God's word from coming to pass by harming God's people.

When the devil tried to kill all the Hebrew boys in Egypt during the days of Moses, the devil was trying to stop God's word from being fulfilled. Satan did the same thing in the days of Jesus's birth, attempting to kill all the Hebrew boys, using the reign of King Herod.

This shows us the devil has been working on his schemes for thousands of years and he still has not succeeded in his efforts. The devil is not wise and all knowing like God. He has limited power, knowledge, and ability. Satan knows what the scripture says, and he tries to stop the scripture from coming to pass, but history proves he cannot do that. He doesn't have the authority and power to alter or change God's word.

If the devil can manipulate the scriptures and deceive people into believing him more than they believe God, he can use those people to do evil and perpetuate his plans. The devil's plan has been the same from the beginning. Satan steals, twists, and manipulates God's creation and God's word to attempt to defeat God. But this is a battle he will never win, because God says the battle is already done and Satan is a defeated foe.

Satan wants to win the war against God because he wants to prevent being thrown into the lake of fire. Revelation 20:10 says, *"And the devil, who deceived them, was thrown into the lake of burning sulfur, where the beast and the false prophet had been thrown. They will be tormented day and night for ever and ever."* (AMPC)

As Jesus died on the cross for the world's sin, He did so to delegate the authority and the power over Satan to His Church. Jesus died for believers to be separate from unbelievers and to share in the divine nature of Christ, permitting them to escape all of the curses of the law.

Matthew 28:18 declares, *"Then Jesus came to them and said, 'All authority in heaven and on the earth has been given to me. Therefore, go and make disciples of all nations, baptizing them in the name of the Father and the Son and the Holy Spirit, and teaching them to obey everything I have commanded you. And surely, I am with you always, to the very end of the age.'"* (AMPC)

So many wonderful stories, like the story of David, were written about the believers in the Old Testament. These believers lived lives of supernatural protection, provision, and abundance before Jesus was crucified and resurrected, because God's Spirit was still present with them. But, with the power of the new covenant, the Church is stronger than it has ever been.

Believers today regardless of their race, gender, age, or background have a better covenant with better promises because of the sacrifice of Jesus Christ, and with our better covenant we can do all things through Him who gives us strength. Hebrews 8:6 tells us, *"But as it is, Christ has acquired a [priestly] ministry which is more excellent [than the old Levitical priestly ministry], for He is the Mediator (Arbiter) of a better covenant [uniting God and man], which has been enacted and rests on better promises."* (AMPC)

The modern church has the inner dwelling of the Holy Spirit. We have full access to heaven and the scriptures tell us we are seated with Christ in the heavens. Through our union with Christ, we have received the keys to the kingdom and full access to the Father.

Our union with Christ and the divine power we have been given allows us to escape the problems and issues of the flesh. The earth and everyone and everything on it can not stand against us. The Holy Spirit allows us to live in the supernatural realm, where we can commune with God and receive provision from Him for everything we need pertaining to life and godliness.

Second Peter 1:3–4 teaches us, *"For His divine power has bestowed on us [absolutely] everything necessary for a [dynamic spiritual] life and godliness, through true and personal knowledge of Him who called us by His own glory and excellence. For by these He has bestowed on us His precious and magnificent promises [of inexpressible value], so that by them you may escape the immoral freedom that is in the world because of disreputable desire and become sharers of the divine nature."* (AMPC)

The word testament means covenant. A covenant is an agreement that has been made between two parties. God had a covenant with His people in the Old Testament, and when Jesus was crucified and resurrected, God made a new covenant with His people. The new covenant gifted His people with both power and with authority on the earth. The new covenant gives us the right to rebuke sickness and disease and to rebuke evil spirits. It gives us the right to command and control anyone and anything that tries to stop us from completing our assignment.

Acts 13:11 teaches us, *"Now the hand of the Lord is against you. You are going to be blind for a time, not even able to see the light of the sun."* Immediately mist and darkness came over him, and he groped about, seeking someone to lead him by the hand. Paul had the power and the authority to rebuke and bring judgment on the sorcerers and the enemies of God using his new covenant rights. He was not overcome by sorcery, for God ordained that this demonic individual would be subordinate to him. *"You are a child of the devil and an enemy of everything that is right! You are full of all kinds of deceit and trickery. Will you never stop perverting the right ways of the Lord?"* (Acts 13:10, NIV)

Both the old and the new covenants separate light from darkness, good from evil, clean and unclean, and believers and unbelievers. In the old covenant, the believers were protected supernaturally from the curses that come onto unbelievers through faith in God's word and promise of protection. Deuteronomy 7:15 explains, *"The Lord will take away from you all sickness; and He will not subject you to any of the harmful diseases of Egypt which you have known, but He will impose them on all [those] who hate you."* (AMPC)

In the new covenant, believers have the promise and the word of the Lord for personal deliverance, and they also have the authority and the power to deliver others from their affliction and their captivity. In addition, the Church has more power than ever to proclaim and enforce God's decrees regarding the enemies of the gospel. Those who pervert the way of justice will receive their God given curse for their behavior, but we must be willing to enforce God's decrees and operate within our proper place as God's ambassadors.

Commitment to the Lord's work, plans, pursuits, and purposes is essential to living a supernatural life, and defeating the works of the flesh and the works of the devil. Each believer must have a love of God and a hatred of the devil alive within them. David was committed to seeing God's plans come forth. Likewise, today, believers need to have a burning desire to destroy the enemy and his kingdom through the power of the Holy Ghost.

Believers need to desire to crucify their own flesh, so they can walk in the Spirit. Galatians 5:16 teaches us, *"But I say, walk habitually in the [Holy] Spirit [seek Him and be responsive to His guidance], and then you will certainly not carry out the desire of the sinful nature [which responds impulsively without regard for God and His precepts]."* (AMPC)

Jesus spoke a lot about commitment and being wholeheartedly committed to the kingdom of God. Committed soldiers are sold out to the cause and will stop at nothing to see their kingdom prevail and conquer. A committed soldier is enlisted to win and to see victories abound. Soldiers don't want to lose, and they refuse to compromise, or back down even when they are surrounded by enemy forces.

Jesus said, *"And whoever does not carry their cross and follow me cannot be my disciple. Suppose one of you wants to build a tower. Won't you first sit down and estimate the cost to see if you have enough money to complete it? For if you lay the foundation and are not able to finish it, everyone who sees it will ridicule you, saying, 'this person began to build and wasn't able to finish.' Or suppose a king is about to go to war against another king. Won't he first sit down and consider whether he is able with ten thousand men to oppose the one coming against him with twenty thousand? If he is not able, he will send a delegation while the other is still a long way off and will ask for terms of peace. In the same way, those of you who do not give up everything you have cannot be my disciples. Salt is good, but if it loses its saltiness, how can it be salty again? It is fit neither for the soil or the manure pile; it is thrown out. Whoever has ears to hear, let them hear"* (Luke 14:27–35, NIV).

When we accept Jesus, we join God's kingdom, and we become a part of God's army. God expects a loyal, unwavering commitment to the kingdom of light. Traitors are people who have no faithfulness and are disloyal. Traitors betray friends, countries, and principles, because they will not wholeheartedly commit to a cause or an obligation. Spiritual traitors are people have a duty to stand with Jesus but choose to compromise, retreat, and negotiate terms with the devil.

Double-minded individuals do not remain loyal to either side of the war. Instead, they try to appease or please both sides, and as a result, no one respects them. Disloyal to both kingdoms, traitors are thrown out and are worth nothing to either side. The lack of commitment and a cowardly nature brings forth ridicule and shame as Jesus promised in Luke 14: *"For if you lay the foundation and are not able to finish it, everyone who sees it will ridicule you, saying, 'this person began to build and wasn't able to finish"* (Amplified).

Judas was a traitor to the kingdom. Although Judas had a call to stand with Jesus, he refused to do so. Judas cared about being accepted by the Pharisees and wanted to be accepted in both camps. Ultimately, Judas hung as a traitor, and his shame was immense. A refusal to wholeheartedly commit and serve the Lord while resisting the enemy resulted in Judas' humiliation and his destruction.

Matthew 27:1–5 shows us Judas' cowardly nature and his impending shame. *"Early in the morning, all the chief priests and the elders of the people made their plans how to have Jesus executed. So, they bound him, led him away and handed him over to Pilate the governor. When Judas, who had betrayed him, saw that Jesus was condemned, he was seized with remorse and returned the thirty pieces of silver to the chief priests and the elders.*

"'I have sinned,' he said, "for I have betrayed innocent blood.'

"'What is that to us?' they replied. 'That's your responsibility.' So, Judas threw the money into the temple and left. Then he went away and hanged himself." (NIV)

A coward is often thought of as someone who is fearful, timid, and weak. By this definition, a coward is a person who is afraid to fight. The Bible says we are to fight the good fight of faith. When people refuse to fight and operate in the power, and instead choose to cower to the devil, it is a serious offense to Jesus Christ, who gave His life for the Church to receive His power and His authority. Revelation 21:8 says, *"But as for the cowardly, the faithless, the detestable, immoral, sorcerers, idolaters, and all liars, their portion will be in the lake that burns with fire and sulfur, which is the second death."* (NIV)

The opposite of a coward is a loyalist. Loyalists remain faithful to their established ruler, kingdom, or government. Loyalists have an allegiance and a commitment to their leader, and they stand with their leader, no matter the price.

Being loyal to God and being loyal to His word are the foundational components of receiving the blessings of the Lord. Faithfulness and a loyalty to God are fruits of the Spirit. With the help of the Holy Spirit, God's people can remain faithful to Him.

The Church's authority, stemming from our partnership with the Lord, makes us fully capable to manifest God's will onto the earth. There is no justification for compromise, or any rationale for failing to fulfill God's purposes under the new covenant. Matthew 16:18 says, *"And I say to you that you are Peter, and on this rock, I will build my church; and the gates of Hell and death will not overpower it."* (NIV) When the devil gains access and dominion over the believer, he has done this through the compromise of their integrity. These people choose to coward to Satan. They have chosen to be a traitor to God.

God must be prioritized in our lives. When He instructs us to treat one another with love and respect, it is a command rather than a suggestion. We honor God by upholding His word. Furthermore, we should remain steadfast in our loyalty to our King and His kingdom by diligently collaborating with those who have also been saved and called, so we can see our kingdom advance and take ground from Satan.

God wants people to rule and reign as His coheirs. God wants to equip us with all wisdom, understanding, and truth, but we must decide to fear the Lord, accept Christ, and submit to learning and living our lives in accordance to His ways and His word. When we decide that we need God and His wisdom more than we need anything else, then we will find the path to life.

Joshua 24:15 says, *"And if it seems evil unto you to serve the Lord, choose you this day whom ye will serve; whether the gods which your fathers served that were on the other side of the flood, or the gods of the Amorites, in whose land ye dwell: but as for me and my house, we will serve the Lord."* (AMPC)

People who do not serve the Lord are serving other gods. People serve the kingdom of light or the kingdom of darkness. People are blessed or cursed. If a voice that isn't God's voice is given an opportunity to rule and reign on the platform in our lives, that voice becomes king and will reign in our lives, and for many people if they are proud they become a god to their self.

Believing oneself to be inherently superior due to gender, race, financial status or other qualifier is a notion that stems from the demonic realm. Such beliefs are not rooted in divine teachings and do not reflect the characteristics of God's Spirit. These teachings have to be rejected and rebuked to have God's blessing, because if you are committed to harming others within God's house you can never walk with God's blessing. First John 4:8 explains, *"The one who does not love has not become acquainted with God [does not and never did know Him], for God is love. [He is the originator of love, and it is an enduring attribute of His nature.]"* (AMPC)

Being blessed is a choice. Being cursed is also a choice. We can choose to keep God's commands or we can choose to disregard them. Proverbs 29:6 states, *"In the transgression of an evil man there is a snare, but the [uncompromisingly] righteous man sings and rejoices. "*

God's kingdom plans can only become second to the plan of the enemies' kingdom when people don't resist the devil and make him flee from their lives. James 4:7 tells us, *"Submit yourself to God. Resist the devil and he will flee."* (NIV)

Submitting to God is submitting to His word, His plan, and His way. Submitting to God means placing God's kingdom pursuits over the pursuits of the enemy forces. Submitting to God means having faith for the impossible and believing in things that are unseen—and refusing to back down, even when you are surrounded. Psalms 23:4 declares, *"Even though I walk through the [sunless] valley of the shadow of death, I fear no evil, for You are with me; Your rod [to protect] and Your staff [to guide], they comfort and console me."* (AMPC)

Believers must take every thought captive into obedience with God's word. We must cast down all wrong thoughts and belief systems. We fight the good fight of faith by choosing to hate and reject evil, lies, and sin, and actively resisting the enemy forces. Upon accepting Jesus Christ as our Savior, we are enlisted to fight and stand firm against the devil's kingdom. *"We are destroying sophisticated arguments and every exalted and proud thing that sets itself up against the [true] knowledge of God, and we are taking every thought and purpose captive to the obedience of Christ"* (Second Corinthians 10:5, Amplified).

Renewing the human mind is an intentional act. The human mind is separate from the Spirit, and it must be consistently renewed. To succeed on the earth, a Christian must commit himself or herself to the study of, and the obedience of, God's word, because God's word is the only thing that renews the human mind. As we renew our minds, we become equipped and knowledgeable about how to be loyal to God's purposes, plans, and pursuits, and diligent in the work of the destruction of darkness.

Proverbs 14:12 teaches, *"There is a way that seems right to a man, but its end is the way of death."* (NIV) To avoid the path of destruction and death, we must consciously choose to walk the path of light and life by receiving divine revelation from God's Word.

Divine revelation comes from the Spirit showing and illuminating truth and lies. When we receive divine revelation, we can see things that we could not see before, and we know the difference between God's voice and the enemy's voice. Through revelation of God's word, the Lord removes any spiritual blindness, so we can navigate and proceed in the direction we are to go.

There is a way that seems appealing or correct to the natural senses and the natural man, but that way often leads to problems and destruction. Faith requires us to look deeper than our physical senses and look to the Spirit for help and guidance above everything else. When we look to God for His divine perspective and revelation, we can have faith that we are walking on the path of life.

Faith doesn't have to make sense to our minds. We don't have to use our physical senses and intellect to determine the truths of God. Relying too heavily on the human understanding and the human senses will lead us astray, so we must never use these things as our guide. Hebrews 11:1 says, *"Faith is the assurance (title deed, confirmation) of things hoped for (divinely guaranteed), and the evidence of things not seen [the conviction of their reality- faith comprehends as fact what cannot be experienced by the physical senses.]"* (AMPC)

Victory belongs to the child of God because Jesus bought that victory on the cross. To defeat the devil, we must have the deed of the assurance of the ownership and possession of our victory stored in our minds and in our hearts. When we have the title to something we know it is ours.

To walk in victory we must know what we have been given and never stop fighting to keep our inheritance even when the devil or others in the world try to stop us from being able to access it. All believers have a covenant right to experience blessing and victory because we were born again into God's family. The new birth granted access to all the family heirlooms and blessings. The new birth provided everything that we need for success.

Christians don't have to beg for their inheritance because the inheritance has already been granted through our relationship to the Father and the Son! A newborn baby doesn't have to beg his or her parents for a crib, clothes, or food to eat, because parents willingly provide everything out of love.

Likewise, the believer doesn't have to beg God for help and victory in his or her life. God has already provided His children with everything that they need to be successful. God has already defeated the devil. Christians are on the winning side. There is not a power struggle between God and the devil.

God is the ultimate boss. He is the ultimate ruler. God has unmatched power, authority, dominion, and influence. When we were born again, we joined a family that is superior in all things. Our title deed of success over the devil and all who do his work belongs to us if we simply believe!

The devil wants to steal the title deed and the assurance of our family heirlooms through lies and deception. Satan attempts to conceal the truth from the Church, and he attempts to convince people that God's word is not true for them, because it is his only chance of success. It is only through a great deception that the devil can have power and dominion over a born-again, spirit-filled Christian.

And that is why God tells us to feed and refresh even our enemies, because when we give all people the right to hear God's word, we feed them and we refresh them, and then they can choose who they will make an alliance with. They choose if they will accept God's message, or if they will continue in the works of the Evil One.

"To the contrary, "Beloved, never avenge yourselves, but leave it to the wrath of God, for it is written, "Vengeance is mine, I will repay, says the Lord." if your enemy is hungry, feed him; if he is thirsty, give him something to drink; for by so doing you will heap burning coals on his head" (Romans 12:19-20, NIV).

Food and refreshment from God for His people or for His enemies only comes from preaching the full counsel of God. We must pierce people with the sword of the Spirit confronting them in their hearts. We must draw blood as commanded in Jeremiah 48. We can never worship man or woman and crave their approval and acceptance. Instead, we must love all people enough to attempt to save their souls from destruction by giving them a chance to repent, be saved, and live righteous through Christ.

In order to experience blessing and success in this life and the next, we must have a personal relationship with Jesus Christ. Like all title deeds and legal inheritances, people gain access to their inheritance through a personal relationship with another individual. Without the relationship, there is no inheritance. We must have a personal and intimate relationship with God the Father, through Jesus Christ the Son, to receive blessings and our inheritance from God.

It is promised that unbelievers and backsliders will see the blessing that God has placed on our lives. There is a noticeable difference between the Christian and the unbeliever. People can tell when we have been with Jesus.

Unbelievers and traitors may temporarily experience success in the world, but they will suffer along with their success. Unbelievers must toil and work hard to achieve in life, and when success is achieved, they still experience suffering, especially when they position themselves against God's agenda. These people will lose everything, because they made the wrong alliance.

Men like Nabal, Goliath, and Saul had money, physical strength and stature, political power, and prestige, but they didn't have the blessing of God. Nothing is more important than the blessing of the Lord, and the wise man knows it!

"The blessing of the Lord brings [true] riches, And He adds no sorrow to it [for it comes as a blessing from God]. Engaging in evil is like a sport to the fool [who refuses wisdom and chases sin], But to a man of understanding [skillful and godly] wisdom brings joy. What the wicked fears will come upon him, But the desire of the righteous [for the blessings of God] will be granted. When the whirlwind passes, the wicked is no more, But the righteous has an everlasting foundation" (Proverbs 10:22–25, Amplified)

IF YOU HAVE NEVER ACCEPTED JESUS CHRIST AS YOUR LORD AND SAVIOR PRAY THE SALVATION PRAYER.

Dear Heavenly Father,

I admit that I am a sinner. I know I have sinned against you. I don't want to be a sinner anymore, and I do not want to go to a devil's hell. Today, I come before you in the name of Jesus, Your Son, and I ask for you to forgive me of all of my sin. Wipe away my sin and make me a new creature. Come into my heart and change me. I ask for your Holy Spirit to guide me into all truth for the rest of my life. Let me never ignore or grieve the Spirit, but let me hear and see the truth and then be quick to follow and obey. I thank you the sacrifice you made on my behalf. You said if I believe in my heart and confess with my mouth that Jesus is Lord then I will be saved. I receive that salvation today. I confess I am a child of God enlisted to serve and honor You forever.

In Jesus name I pray. Amen.

The Bible verses have been sourced from a variety of Biblical sources:

(Amplified Classic Bible)

(English Standard Version Bible)

(New International Version Bible)

(New King James Version Bible)

(New Living Translation Bible)

United States Senate. (n.d.). *Constitution of the United States*. Senate.gov. https://www.senate.gov/about/origins-foundations/senate-and-constitution/constitution.htm

www.ingramcontent.com/pod-product-compliance
Lightning Source LLC
Chambersburg PA
CBHW070919130626
46555CB00001B/198